33voices on Entrepreneurship

Startup Success Secrets from Thought Leaders

By Moe Abdou

Copyright © Moe Abdou, 2014

All rights reserved.

Contents

Contents ii

Introduction v

Section 1: Finding Big Ideas 1

    Chapter 1:   Going with the Flow 2

    Chapter 2:   Finding Big Ideas 5

    Chapter 3:   Staying True to Your Roots 11

    Chapter 4:   Making People Happy 17

    Chapter 5:   Taking Action 22

    Chapter 6:   Getting Things to Grow 27

    Chapter 7:   Piquing Investor Interest 32

    Chapter 8:   Discovering Your Customers' Needs 37

    Chapter 9:   Hooking Your Customers 42

    Chapter 10: Making Little Bets 47

    Chapter 11: Evolving a Startup 53

Section 2: Pivot or Persevere 57

    Chapter 12: Stacking the Odds in Your Favor 58

    Chapter 13: Having an "I'll Figure it Out" Attitude 62

    Chapter 14: Thriving 67

Chapter 15: **Cultivating Serendipity** 72

Chapter 16: **Driving Startup Success** 78

Chapter 17: **Fighting Fear** 83

Chapter 18: **Living Fearlessly** 88

Chapter 19: **Taking a Few Turns** 92

Chapter 20: **Riding Prosperity Cycles** 97

Chapter 21: **Tracking Metrics That Matter** 103

Chapter 22: **Leading Ethically** 108

Section 3: Leading People 113

Chapter 23: **Empowering Others** 114

Chapter 24: **Tapping Hidden Talent** 120

Chapter 25: **Trying Before You Buy** 125

Chapter 26: **Creating a Collaborative Culture** 130

Chapter 27: **Feeding a Hungry Startup** 135

Chapter 28: **Creating a Job to Keep a Job** 139

Chapter 29: **Embracing Social Change** 143

Chapter 30: **Protecting Your Assets** 149

Chapter 31: **Thinking Like Zuck** 155

Chapter 32: **Acquiring a Practical Education** 159

Chapter 33: **Going All-In** 164

About the Author 170

Introduction

Nearly 25 years ago, I started successfully coaching financial professionals serving the wealth management needs of emerging entrepreneurs in Washington, D.C. In doing this, I strove to understand far more than the financial aspects of my clients' businesses. It was my overwhelming belief that if I could help these clients solve their internal problems, then their financial challenges would easily be addressed.

To find out how to do that at scale and with meaningful impact, I conducted a small experiment. On the first Friday in January 2000, I invited twenty-five promising entrepreneurs together for an informal lunch gathering to discuss the workplace of the future. There was no selling, no presentation, and no fixed agenda ... only unfiltered dialogue on how to design a creative work environment that would attract and inspire the brightest talent.

There was no shortage of aha-moments during that first session driven solely by the power of deliberate and meaningful conversation. None of us are smarter than all of us. The entrepreneurs, my team, and I walked away knowing that work as we knew it was about to take a radical turn.

Since that day, I focused the next chapter of my life on discovering new ways for entrepreneurs to think, grow, and live. While there is no more valuable guide than experience, entrepreneurs accelerate their success and avoid mistakes by drawing upon the wisdom of the explorers who came before them.

My small experiment grew into 33voices, a knowledge network that exists to help entrepreneurs succeed faster. I do that by promoting progressive ideas and the thought leaders who deliver them. In late 2009, I collaborated with 33 influential thinkers to highlight the ideas each felt were about to shape the upcoming decade. The result was our first digital anthology - Elevate - which not only shared their imagination, but also has inspired an ongoing dialogue with more than 650 of the world's foremost authorities on business and life.

This book is my way of giving you practical techniques and new ways of thinking to help you tackle any business startup problems. To help you accomplish this feat, I present the insights of 33 progressive thinkers and doers grouped into three sections that mirror the primary determinates of entrepreneurial success: Finding Big Ideas, Pivoting or Persevering, and Leading People.

The experience of these individuals proves there is no single formula for success – only the one that works for you. My advice is to read how others achieved their dreams and glean from them what could work for you. Don't be afraid to cherry-pick. You don't need to adopt one philosophy wholesale; use advice that resonates as a jumping off point to formulate your own plan.

I hope that reading each epiphany makes you a little smarter and a lot faster. Good luck!

Section 1:
Finding Big Ideas

Chapter 1

Going with the Flow

When I think of Guy Kawasaki, I think of a model entrepreneur, an accomplished investor, and a world-class thinker—yet today, his name is most synonymous with social media. Spend one day following his social stream and you'll feel like you've known him for years. His millions of evangelists, including myself, follow him because he's always genuine, never phony, and is forever seeing the world with a fresh pair of eyes. To him, social media is hard work, very personal, and of course, an enchanting way to magnetize your brand. Although he's an active contributor to the major social networks, here's why Google+ is his network of choice.

Guy Kawasaki

Guy Kawasaki is a special advisor to the Motorola business unit of Google. Previously, he was the chief evangelist of Apple. He is also the author of <u>APE</u>, <u>What the Plus!</u>, <u>Enchantment</u>, and nine other books. Kawasaki earned his BA from Stanford University and an MBA from UCLA, and received an honorary doctorate from Babson College.

I strive to empower with my writing, my speaking, my investing, and my advising. Although working for Steve Jobs greatly influenced the way I think, my first real job, working for a jewelry company is what shaped me. There, I learned how to sell in a difficult retail environment. All this highfalutin MBA, investment bank, business development kind of stuff -- it's all B.S. compared to selling retail which comes down to three things: trust, likability, and competence.

If I could design a startup school for students of entrepreneurship, I would create a three- or four- month course covering the basics of how things work in business. Students would learn why to incorporate, how to interact with the board of directors, and how to pitch an idea in 30 seconds. I want you to know the basics of human resources – what you can and cannot do in an interview, to keep you out of jail and on the ethical path. That's it.

Then I would just get people out there, telling them to start building what they want to sell, because prototyping is the most important step. As someone who gets pitched prototypes constantly, I think the ability to recognize good ideas relies on gut instinct. And, I hate to tell you, but your gut is wrong half the time. At any given point, you think you know. Sometimes you're right, and you only remember those. Most of the time you're wrong, and you forget those and you blame that on somebody else. That's how it really works.

When somebody is pitching me, I prefer the 10/20/30 model – 10 slides, 20 minutes, 30 point font. I think 10 slides forces you to really get to the point, while providing lots of time to show your prototype. Unfortunately, I'm still getting many 100-page plans.

Marketing at a startup can be very lean. A tech startup today needs infrastructure, but can get all that through cloud services. You don't need to buy servers anymore. You need marketing, but you use Twitter, Facebook, Google+, LinkedIn, and Pinterest for that. You need people, but people are cheaper and don't need to be in the same physical location because they are all virtual. Tools are all open source, so the tools, the marketing, the people, the commercial real estate, the infrastructure, all of that is free or cheap.

I love the social media component of marketing and I think it is actually pretty simple. Decide on a positioning, branding, or niche that you want to occupy as an expert. From then on, curate content that positions you in that niche and disseminate it as widely as possible. Fix up your profile, include a picture or video with your posts, and keep adding to it.

80% of my effort goes manually into Google+, and then virtual assistants deploy that in other places. I like Google+ the most, so most of my action is Google+.

What people need to understand about Google+ is that each service has a different primary purpose. Twitter is for fleeting "perceptions". Facebook is for "people." Pinterest is for "pinning" pictures and nothing more.

Google+ is for "passions." These are people you don't necessarily know yet, but who share your passion for photography or for adoption or for food. You may have these passions, but people in your life, like your classmates or your relatives, don't share them. You stay on Facebook to just share the same old stuff with the same old people. But, you go to Google+ to find new people who share your passions.

I'm unusual in that my business is to be in social media. Social media for me is not something fun; it's a means to an end. It's part of what I do as my function. I spend two or three hours a day on social media, but it's not clear that everybody can do that. Perhaps the secret to my success is that I'm willing to work harder than most at it.

Chapter 2

Finding Big Ideas

The making of a brand is lifetime endeavor. It's one that starts by deeply connecting with your values and lives on when they move others.

A good friend shared a restaurant experience recently that captured that essence for me. During a recent visit to the fashionable NoMad restaurant in New York City, he engaged his waiter in sharing the philosophy behind the uber-cool NoMad brand. His waiter opted instead for show and tell, and walked Patrick to the kitchen where he showed him a framed white portrait with 11 words meticulously positioned on it, including: Loose, Alive, Enduring, Original, Thoughtful and Satisfaction. He went on to explain that each of their restaurants is distinguished by a unique theme with this one being The Rolling Stones. "That's what we stand for, and every action any of us takes serves one of those eleven words." Brand maven Debra Kaye tells me that "a brand is a personality," and in her latest book, *Red Thread Thinking*, she explains why "everything old is new."

Debra Kaye

Debra Kaye authored <u>Red Thread Thinking</u> and shares the book's insights on creating and sustaining innovation by using what she calls the "five threads."

The books I read about innovation all described how to bring an already discovered innovation to market, but did not tell me how to start and where to get ideas when you have an empty head. That's what I needed to figure out and what I want to share.

I wanted people to admit: "I have no idea where to get an idea. Give me techniques that show me where to look for insights." The five 'threads' I identified are places one can look to formulate ideas. They provide a solution when you don't know where to begin and you're looking at that scary blank piece of paper.

The first red thread, "Innovation -- It's All in Your Head" is meant to give you the confidence, to help you open up your mind, to understand you're never too old to innovate, and to show you how to free up your mind and relax and say that you can do it. The best thing I like to tell anyone to do is to change your mindset. When we were growing up, we all heard about the power of positive thinking. There is nothing greater than the power of positive thinking when it comes to innovation. Let me give you two examples.

The first is that if we think we're smarter, we're actually going to be smarter. You've heard that when athletes visualize winning, it really helps them win. Being smart is the same thing. If you think you're smart, you're actually going to be smarter. So, first you need to have confidence in your abilities to be creative.

The second example relates to a concept known as functional fixedness - the notion that, especially as we get older, and lose that sense of child-like wonder, we start to limit and restrict ourselves. For instance, let's say you're walking through a forest and a burr falls on your sweater. You think, "Gosh, this burr, it's really a pain" and you pull it off your sweater, throw it to the ground, and continue walking. The next time that happens to you, instead of just pulling this burr off your sweater, think of it positively. Look at this burr and say, "Wow! That's really interesting. How did this burr come to stick on my sweater? What caused it to stay stuck? Isn't that interesting? I wonder how that happened." And file that away. That's a pattern. And, in the future when ... somebody might need something that sticks to a piece of paper or somebody needs something that sticks to a wall, your mind will remember the memory of that burr that stuck to your sweater, and you just might invent the next Velcro.

The second red thread is "Everything Old Is New Again." This thread is about showing you one of the places you can look to find new ideas. Do you have technology that is old? Think about how you might retool that technology. Have you given up on concepts that aren't working? Revisit those concepts because maybe they did not work simply because you looked at them in a limited way.

Another technique is to see through fresh eyes. If somebody new comes into your business, perhaps even a young intern, sit them down before they assimilate. Let them take a look at your original development plans and data. They may uncover new information and new patterns of great value that you missed.

Red thread number three is "Consumers – The Strangest Animals at the Zoo." Look at the way people do things. Just watch the way your wife jury-rigs something at home because it's not quite working for her. That's an innovation waiting to happen.

When you're innovating, you have tons of information in front of you and this can make it very, very difficult to discern which information is important and which is not. The critical factor here is knowing that no one single piece of information is ever important. What I suggest is to look for repeating patterns to guide your way.

Apple is brilliant at this. When they wanted to develop a new MP3 player, they could have done what technology companies traditionally did and said, "I want to come out with a better looking _____," but they didn't. Instead, they watched people to figure out how people wanted to get, manage, and listen to their music. Instead of just creating a better MP3 player, they created iTunes. They created a way to get rid of painful and technically complex steps consumers had to take to get music on an MP3 player. Apple looked at music as the end benefit, rather than a more beautiful MP3 player, and now they own 80% of all downloaded music.

People have the misguided sense that consumer behaviors and cultures change very rapidly. We hear of all these new trends in the media, but actually change happens slowly. When we're talking about brands, instead of saying, 'Oh my God, I have to change my brand because this is the newest trend,' innovate on the basis of underlying human behaviors. That's how your product or service is going to be enduring.

Consider the billions of dollars that have been spent on the 'anti-smoking' campaign aimed at young people with little real impact. You can tell people that smoking is going to kill them, but dying is not prominent in their minds; it's not something they can relate to when they are healthy and young. Instead, the campaign must be about something that really rings true.

We did a non-smoking campaign, targeted at teenagers in Latin America, that was really effective and we never talked about death or dying. We actually got 20% of the teenagers to stop smoking. We told them, "Guess what? Go ahead, smoke if you want to. But, you know what? If you smoke your hair is going to stink, your teeth are going to turn yellow, and you might get wrinkles ten years earlier than all your friends. And then, because you're a little smelly your friends might not accept you as much." And the printed warning on the package of cigarettes said, "Smoking seriously endangers your looks" instead of "smoking seriously endangers your health." We were playing into their need to fit in.

Red thread number four is "What You See Is What You Get." Sometimes it's the simplest fix. Consider how often innovative new ideas are packaged in the same old familiar packaging. If you have a cereal with a new ingredient in it and you package like the old one, no one will know. If it looks like a duck and talks like a duck, package it like a duck. Don't package it like a chicken as everyone else has done.

The fifth and final red thread is "The Force of Passion." If you're not passionate and loving it, then you're not going to be able to sell it to investors or to the public. To instill passion in others, make sure there is a real product difference in your product, something of real value, more than a mere marketing gimmick. Once you've distinguished your product from the others, don't muck it up by confusing the issue. Make that one difference obvious in your packaging. Make it obvious in your communications. If you focus on too many things, then it's hard for consumers to discern what you're really trying to say.

Those are the "five red threads" for creating and sustaining innovation.

Chapter 3

Staying True to Your Roots

Building a business is always personal. The most successful startups tend to be built on purpose and almost always mirror the ideals of its founders. When Andrew Geant and Michael Weishuhn dreamed of building Wyzant, a marketplace for tutors, they started with the premise that although tutoring was here to stay, great tutors were especially difficult to find. Further, they understood that modern society has influenced parents to act with greater caution when inviting strangers around their kids. So they did what most successful entrepreneurs do—LISTEN. They certainly had the proverbial big idea, but their early success was anchored by their decision to stay local. They quickly built a prototype and in 2005, they started experimenting in their home base—the Washington DC area. It was a two-man show for almost three years, with Mike handling everything web and programming related and Andrew juggling everything else. What they didn't know, they learned along the way and their greatest lessons emerged from customer feedback.

Today, they have over 60,000 tutors, 42 employees, and are one of the most respected educational portals on the web. What's most impressive to me is their decision to stay private and not accept outside capital. Here's their business building philosophy.

Andrew Geant

WyzAnt Tutoring co-founder and CEO Andrew Geant shows how to start, and expand, a homegrown venture.

After graduating from college in 2005, I started WyzAnt to do some math tutoring. Even though I was a pretty savvy web user, I quickly realized I did not know how to promote my services. So, I brought in my co-founder and CIO Mike Weishuhn, one of my computer science friends from college, to add his technical expertise and to brainstorm with. We came up with a somewhat obvious idea – let's build a marketplace for tutoring. At the time, it was somewhat revolutionary because nothing like it existed.

I realize that people will question using the Internet to find a tutor to work with their child in their own home. In 2005, that was certainly a common concern – the Internet was okay for e-commerce, but it was not perceived as a reliable place to find somebody who could be entrusted to work with your child. Yet, Mike and I never wavered, because it was second nature for us to turn to the Internet for everything. And the public has caught up: our growth has been fueled by people becoming more comfortable going online and searching for things like tutoring and home services.

Our business model is almost exactly the same as when we started. Many entrepreneurs start building a community, and then a few years later ask themselves how they are going to make money. In contrast, we had to start with a viable business model because we had no money of our own and no outside capital.

Mike and I took a very methodical approach. Starting out on a very local level in Northern Virginia was probably one of the smartest things we did. We recruited tutors to our website while simultaneously recruiting parents and students. Because we stayed small, we were able to learn a lot about what worked and what didn't, and then improve the product before expanding. Soon we spread out to all of metropolitan Washington, D.C. Next, we recruited tutors in New York City, Los Angeles, and Chicago. In just a few years, we had gone national.

The second smart thing we did was not rushing to hire. At the very beginning, we were pounding the pavement in true guerilla fashion. Our pitch to tutors was easy. We initially focused on college, university, and graduate students ... smart individuals who needed money. Once we built the platform, however, we realized there was no reason to restrict to just college and graduate students, so we expanded the pool of potential tutors.

On the parent side, our pitch was initially a little more difficult. Again, we had to overcome the sensitivity to hiring a tutor online. We helped break down those barriers by talking at length to parents over the phone and providing a very personal experience; back then, we were heavily involved in every match. Once our credibility spread by good word-of-mouth, we did not have to get involved in the thousands of individual transactions.

Role and responsibility assignment was really easy because Mike and I had such different skills. I'm not a developer, so there was no way I was going to build our website. It was very clear from the beginning that Mike would be doing all the frontend and backend web development. Mike has a great outlook toward things he doesn't know how to do; an eager learner, he'll figure those things out.

If you are a non-technical personal starting an online business, you have to get a technical co-founder. That's key. So many entrepreneurs have nightmare stories of outsourcing their development; it's very expensive, inefficient, and rife with communication issues. Get somebody who can do the development and give them equity.

By default, I was the one-man customer service department, the CFO, and the CEO. I was our marketing department and all other non-technical aspects of the business. One of the best things was getting feedback from our initial users whose insights drove our product improvement. To this day, we rely on our customer service department for a lot of our ideas.

For the first three-and-a-half years, Mike and I comprised the entire operation. The amount of time I was putting in answering phones and handling administrative tasks was not making sense anymore. So, despite our efforts to avoid it, we had to bring on someone else. Our first hire was for an entry level position, a personal friend of ours and recent graduate. We didn't go out and try to get some big hotshot C-level person. We started small.

About six months later, I also realized I was not the ideal CFO either. The issues were becoming a little too complicated for me to learn. So, our next hire was our CFO, Brent Johnson. Brent would likely not have joined our company at that time but for the personal connection I was able to establish with an advisor from my Princeton alumni network. This adviser pulled Brent from his Rolodex and vouched for us. I remain convinced that's the only reason we were able to convince a guy who had decades of experience, as a CPA and a former CFO of a proprietary trading firm, to come on board. Although to hear him tell it, our infectious enthusiasm helped, too.

As the company has grown, Mike and I have taken on more strategic roles; we have fun finding ways to add value on a broader level. That being said, we both still like to get in the weeds of big projects coming down the pipeline. I'll still manage projects and work with our designers and Mike still does a lot of coding. In fact, I would be lying if I said it was totally easy to transition from my former jack-of-all-trades role to a more managerial, strategic function. I have had many helpful advisers in the process, but I remain a work in progress.

Although we have evolved to draw in outside talent, we have yet to change our mind about outside funding. In the beginning, we insisted, "we're capable of doing this on our own." However, as we grew and started fielding calls from investors, it has become a little more tempting.

Yet, we've been fortunate enough to have a good cash flow business, enabling us to funnel the funds right back into the company. We really like to go about things our own way. We have an awesome culture; it's just a great place to work. We have our dogs at the office. People wear flip-flops and hoodies. We have full health insurance for all our employees, lunch is provided. We are able to do all this because we don't answer to anybody. I think that is what carries the day every time we stop and consider raising money.

Corporate culture feeds on itself. By getting good people, you get more good people who stay because they are surrounded by quality. In fact, many new hires in our customer service department were referred by existing customer service representatives. We love to grow by internal recommendations. Finding quality programmers can be really difficult. In this regard, being based in Chicago is a big advantage -- we're not competing against the Silicon Valley giants for talent, so we are able to recruit and retain top tier developers.

Our culture has helped sustain our mission. Despite the fact that tutoring is very "old school," it is going to be around forever. Yes, there are many interesting trends in electronic education – gameification, adaptive learning, and MOOCs (massive open online courses). We complement those trends with asynchronous learning and learning management systems. We also believe there is a time and a place for online tutoring, a service we hope to provide in the future. But, at the end of the day, from time to time, everyone needs to sit down with somebody shoulder-to-shoulder, and learn one-on-one.

Chapter 4

Making People Happy

The great distinction of iconoclast entrepreneurs is their relentless pursuit of greatness. Steve Jobs taught us that *better* never stops. He was a design genius obsessed with building insanely great products that empowered us to celebrate our uniqueness. Cut from the same cloth, Tony Hsieh of Zappos is a marketing prodigy who's continually re-imaging the retail experience. He taught us that the path to sustainable profits, passion, and purpose starts with delivering happiness.

Just a few years ago, another aspiring entrepreneur, Ben Huh, made it his goal to make people happy for five minutes each day. What started as the *I Can Has Cheezburger* cat blog that he purchased from friends in 2007 has turned into a media empire with almost 400 million page views a month, a network reality show, a pile of venture money, and an imaginative way to share news. Here's the most important lesson that we can all learn from Ben.

Ben Huh

Ben Huh is a South Korean Internet entrepreneur and the CEO of The Cheezburger Network, which receives 375 million views a month across its 50 sites. He's also a co-founder and board member of Circa, which bills itself as "news, re-imagined."

I didn't have huge dreams. I started out in 2007 when I raised money to buy a site called 'I can has Cheezburger.' I didn't know what the hell I was doing. I had no idea how to run a business. It was just me and my dog. The goal was to live to fight another day. I wanted to generate enough revenue each month to be alive the next month. That was really it – I was living in thirty-day increments.

This company has gone through a very gradual process of expansion. In 2009, I began to see that Internet culture was becoming more and more mainstream. I thought that I needed to bring in a set of investors who wanted to go big, who wanted to take a huge swing at it. I didn't mind risking my money all over again. My original investors wanted to exit, saying "I've already spent all this time with you. We've been successful. Now, I want to take my chips and go home." Fortunately, new investors wanted in.

We raised a total of $37 million dollars by the end of our second venture capital round. With more capital, we decided to reinvent what we do. Internet culture is becoming more and more mainstream. We need to diversify the types of content people can see. We need to have a platform that allows us to extend to mobile and tablets. We had to rethink who we were and what we did as a company -- our technology, product, and content.

I had the necessary perspective from my prior failed startups to understand what that entails. There is nothing harder than waking up in the morning looking in the mirror and seeing failure, knowing that I let people down who had put their faith in me. I recalled a startup I did in 2000, which went away when the dot-com bubble burst. There were 20 investors who each contributed from a few thousand dollars to a hundred thousand dollars. These people trusted me to do my best, but I had so little experience and no idea what I was doing. By 2001, I felt I had let them down because I wasn't a success.

Fast forward, to 2007 when I started Cheezburger ... of course, I still don't want to let my new investors down, but I have a much better perspective of what letting people down means, what doing a startup is all about.

I want to succeed in an ethical and a moral and a professional way. I wear many hats. I'm a founder. I'm an entrepreneur. I'm an investor. I'm an employee. And, I'm a human being, which is my most important role. That's the foundation. You can build a professional career, but nothing changes the fact that you are a human being with responsibilities. You have to wear many hats, and they balance each other out. You can't be a successful entrepreneur if you lie, cheat, and do whatever it takes to get to the top. You need to have boundaries and you need to have investors who support that idea.

What's really important for me to measure our success are the smiles we put on the faces of our users. The world is changing dramatically. We are now the number one humor destination on mobile phones. We never hit number one on desktop in our category, but we've had it for mobile. That's the kind of impact that makes me happy.

I love the line from Forrest Gump: "Life is like a box of chocolates. You never know what you're going to get." Cheezburger is about that surprise. You might not know exactly what you'll get, but you know it's going to be delicious. I think that creates an addictive quality.

It also creates contrast. The contrast stems from the juxtaposition of content; in fact, a lot of the content that people submit to our sites is not laugh-out-loud funny. Some of it is touching. Some of it just makes you smile. Some of it is just awesome. But, it's not just about "standup comedian" style humor. It's about laughter. It's about smiling. It's about serendipity. All those things are what really make our experience fun.

Circa, in contrast to Cheezburger, came about because of personal frustration. I would go to a major news website and I would read the same article over and over again thinking journalism never left Web 1.0. Traditional media players never reinvented themselves because they're used to creating content in a model that is centuries old.

What I wanted to do was to shrink the inefficiency of reading news. One of the huge differentiators of Circa is that you can follow a specific story – not a topic, not a city, not a name. If there is a tornado in Oklahoma and little is known in the first few minutes, you can click the follow button and be notified when the incremental updates happen. What we do is make the process easier so people can follow more stories. People want to be informed without the overhead of reading the same stuff over and over again.

I have a theory about what I call 'native formats.' If you think about the version 1.0 of any technology, it's the previous way of doing business -- just moved to a new platform. Version 1.0 of Internet shopping was a brick and mortar store letting you buy things in the same way, but on the

Internet. Well, version 2.0 and beyond gives people a totally new and different experience using the Internet.

For example, if you want to merely port humor from the old world, it would just be articles, video clips, and TV shows. Well, Cheezburger is more than that. It's about remixing. It's about Internet culture. Circa, too, reinvents the news experience. Experience matters; participation matters. Those are the huge levers we have to pull.

Our mission is to make more and more people happy. We aim to be the household name and brand, the go-to place, when it comes to needing a few minutes of mental vacation.

Chapter 5

Taking Action

Aristotle once said, "For the things we have to learn before we can do them, we learn by doing them." And for entrepreneurs, that's permission to tinker with ideas. It's a mindset that entrepreneurial success is an evolutionary process, and one that will never end. It starts with a small idea and grows into an ongoing experiment that reveals what the marketplace accepts and what we have to change.

Growing up, I was rarely encouraged to take 'the road less traveled.' Instead, my generation was more about conformity and stability. Today, however, that 'road less traveled' might be the only logical path towards a meaningful career. Modern society calls for fresh thinking and inspired action, and when it comes to dealing with an unknowable future, Babson College President Len Schlesinger passionately suggests, "If you can't predict the future—and increasingly you can't—action trumps everything." For decades now, Babson College has been the preeminent school for "entrepreneurship of all kinds," and as it's 12th President, Schlesinger is more determined than ever to teach you their method.

Leonard Schlesinger

Len Schlesinger, author of <u>Just Start</u> and president of Babson College, recognized for 17 consecutive years by <u>U.S. News & World Report</u> as the top school for entrepreneurship in the country, tackles some controversial perceived entrepreneurial wisdom.

I'm hard pressed to declare victory in figuring out the entrepreneurial formula at Babson College. But I do think we've figured out how to use the data we have, on how successful serial entrepreneurs think and act in a variety of settings, to provide a great foundation for young people. This helps not only those who want to be able to start ventures on their own, but also young people who want to dramatically increase their capacity to take effective action in a complex, overwhelming world where most people get paralyzed by their environment. Many in this age group sit around lamenting the fact that the politicians and the experts say this is the first generation that does not have it as good as their parents. What we hope to do is unleash a substantial amount of energy to change that forecast.

There are three things we at Babson believe we know about entrepreneurship, all of which are controversial.

Our first belief is that entrepreneurs are made, not born. The standard belief of countless entrepreneurs is the reverse - entrepreneurs are born, not made. That belief implies there is some genetic underpinning that characterizes people who engage successfully in entrepreneurial activity, and all the rest of us should simply give up. At Babson, we think this is the most depressing scenario to imagine, and, if it were true, there would be DNA-related research to confirm it.

Unfortunately, we celebrate all types of heroes preventing us from thinking about entrepreneurship as an option for everyone. There is no question there are people in the world who are born to be great musicians. And there are people in the world who are born to be great businesspeople. But, I am not particularly interested in a deep understanding of those natural talents, because it cannot be taught to others; it doesn't help me to help anybody else. Rather, I'm interested in understanding people become successful entrepreneurs through a method. Like any other method, it's documentable – consequently, it's teachable to anybody. And the way you actually get good at it is to practice -- the same way a great musician gets to Carnegie Hall. Therefore, we need to provide an environment conducive to practice, which obviously includes an environment for outcomes that are less desirable than what you might have forecasted, namely, failure.

Our second belief is that entrepreneurship is not glamorous. Unintentionally, the stories entrepreneurs spin of themselves don't help. There is a whole portfolio of magazines and books heavily influenced by entrepreneurs who hired ghost writers and conveniently forgot what really happened on the road to success. The stories they tell end up making many people think, "I can't possibly do that." These fanciful tales of swashbuckling risk takers who mortgaged everything, distanced themselves completely from their families, and are hanging by a fingertip from a mountaintop waiting to see if an order comes in, or else they're going to drop and die. The moral: I got the order and am now an entrepreneur, dig me. Those stories don't help at all. The reality is substantially more boring. We wish entrepreneurs were willing to tell the real story about their upward climb in order to engage others in developing an understanding that there is a more mundane method.

Our third belief is that entrepreneurship is a life skill more than a business skill. That method of entrepreneurial action is a way of thinking and acting in the world. In today's highly uncertain environment, as Reid Hoffman of LinkedIn has argued in The Start-up of You, we need to come to grips with the fact that entrepreneurship is a life skill that can assist anybody in a broad variety of settings, regardless of whether their goals are economic or not.

There are three things that prevent people from pursuing entrepreneurial endeavors. First, they hear somebody else's story and decide their idea isn't as good. Second, they get obsessed analytically; they get so attached to their idea they decide now is the time to actually do a detailed business plan. Third, many people actually say they don't have any ideas. That's what I get confronted with most frequently. It's not: "I have an idea and I can't get started." It's: "I don't have a big idea." Well, the answer is you don't have to have a big idea.

In fact, Amar Bhide wrote a book a little over a decade ago on the origins of new business, looking at over 2,000 new ventures and recognizing that 88% of the new ventures were simply extrapolations of ideas that already existed in the marketplace. The vast majority of things that pass for "new" businesses are simply elaborations: doing something a little bit better, bringing something to a different market, bringing something to a different customer segment, or tweaking something.

For example, who would ever think that a great new idea would be to mail customers razorblades every month? Listening to that idea, you suddenly realize that large numbers of men actually don't give much thought to buying razorblades; men don't stockpile them. Our razorblades get dull and when we finally get around to getting a replacement, we can't get the one we want or we can only get it at a local convenience store at an egregious price. So, the notion of simply attacking a regular daily problem with a subscription model has built a substantial business. Is there anything particularly earth-shattering about that idea?

At Babson, we give the opportunity to engage the best characteristics of the scientific method under conditions of uncertainty, which is "I think therefore I test." Instead of thinking about an overwhelming commitment to developing a plan, students figure out a cheap and rapid way test an idea with a portfolio of people. In so doing, they are figuring out whether it's worthwhile to take the next step.

Most business schools and entrepreneurship programs focus completely on the end goal, writing plans about the millions of dollars required to realize your vision. In contrast, I'm lowering the barriers to the next step. Instead of: "What do you want to do?" my question is: "What do you want to do next?" And instead of: "Where are you trying to end up?" the question is really: "What do I want to do with what you have now, and who you are now, and who do you know now?"

I think Harvard's Clay Christensen is understating the case when he posits that there is a 93% chance that your initial business model and strategy will not succeed. If people are being honest, it's almost 100% of the time. That's why I always ask, "Why are you spending so much time on this plan if you actually know with a high degree of reliability that's not going to turn out that way? Why are you developing a deep level of commitment to an approach and to steps way down the road that can't be forecasted without knowing what will happen tomorrow? Instead, focus on a much looser characterization of the steps you're going to take in a much more intentional learning model that will allow you to build the model."

Chapter 6

Getting Things to Grow

Entrepreneurs are dreamers and the best ones always dream of doing what others never thought possible. Turning waste into a gourmet food delicacy is one such idea born out of the ingenuity of two UC Berkeley students, Alejandro Velez & Nikhil Arora, just a few months prior to graduation. In addition to their boundless optimism, what sets this duo apart is their relentless appetite for building a business that matters, and that always starts and ends with the customer.

Observe Alex & Nikhil from a distance and you see two emerging entrepreneurs who understand that "greatness is not a function of circumstances...." as Jim Collins says, "...greatness is largely a matter of conscious choice, and discipline." You'll quickly see why Back To The Roots is destined for greatness.

Nikhil Arora

Back to the Roots' co-founder Nikhil Arora discusses the necessity of a strong partnership, initial distributors' enthusiasm, and knowing when to transition from the tactical to the strategic.

When my business partner Alex Velez and I first started our company, Back to the Roots, as University of California at Berkeley seniors, I was headed for a job in consulting and Alex in investment banking. Despite these very corporate trajectories, we had a passion for education and sustainability, we just did not know how to apply this shared passion after graduation. I had spent six months of my junior year working in Ghana, while Alex had founded what became the largest mentorship program on the UC Berkeley campus.

When we heard about growing gourmet mushrooms on recycled coffee grounds, we got excited by the idea of turning waste into fresh, local food. With respect to our initial pitch, we were clueless, but persistent. First, we took our first ACE Hardware paint bucket of mushrooms to Chez Panisse, a high-end organic restaurant in Berkeley. We met the legendary Alice Waters, the restaurant's founder, and she and her head chef tried some of our mushrooms. We got a confidence boost when the head chef pronounced them delicious.

Later that day, we trotted our pail over to the Berkeley Whole Foods and ended up with eight or nine Whole Foods employees huddled around this one nasty looking paint bucket with a couple of mushrooms. They introduced us to the Northern California Whole Foods regional buyer, Randy, who became one of our closest mentors. Randy's enthusiasm for distributing our product, if we could make it work, gave us the confidence to try.

About a month before graduation, we applied to a Berkeley competition for social innovation, winning a $5,000 grant. But, in the beginning, we couldn't grow a thing. Almost seven months of trial and error passed before we had our first consistent crop. That's when Alex and I realized we worked well together, weathering those initial lowest of lows. We had no clue what we were doing, but we had a blast figuring it out; that was, and still is, the foundation of our partnership. We have tremendous respect for each other, and both of us know we couldn't have made a go of it alone.

To withstand numerous initial failed iterations, it not only helps to have a symbiotic partnership, but also a supportive community. In our case, Whole Foods was the light at the end of the tunnel. Lacking a science background, Alex and I called every mushroom farm trying to get advice; every single one said, "You can't do it on coffee grounds. It's too acidic. It's too dense." But the proof was in front of our eyes in our bucket, we knew it was doable. With that initial proof of concept, we vowed to work backwards to find a scalable and repeatable growing process.

The first year, Alex and I did not assign roles, we just worked together. Our only role at that point was "hustle": no strategy, no marketing. It was just "can we get these things to grow?" We spent that first year knee-deep in coffee grounds. We would drive around collecting coffee grounds, switching off who would drive and who would grab the bags and throw them in the van.

Peet's Coffee, next door to our campus, was the first to give us their grounds. We were fortunate enough to meet (actually, we chased her down) one of the key people at Peet's, at a small conference on sustainability. She understood our passion and what we were trying to accomplish. She became our evangelist at Peet's. We started at a couple of cafes, but when we reached a critical mass of ten, they said, "Let's make this official."

Then, we alternated who pressed the coffee grounds each day and who harvested the mushrooms. That was our life, that's all we did: collect coffee grounds, press them, plant mushroom spawn, harvest mushrooms, and then make sure our product was selling at the Whole Foods evening demonstration. For many months, that was all there was to it.

With respect to business plans, we were winging it, too. At first, we didn't even know we were going to be growing mushrooms. Alex and I thought we might be an intermediary source, collecting coffee grounds and selling them to other mushroom farmers. At some point, we said why not just try growing them ourselves, launching a mushroom kit, and eventually introducing a second product, an aquaponics kit (a fish tank that grows greens).

When we launched the mushroom kit, our business evolved past mere production and into sales, marketing, and customer service. At that point, we delineated roles and responsibilities. We realized we could never expand solely by planting and harvesting all day; we had to be out there marketing and selling. So, our first big hire was in operations, overseeing warehouse and operations. That hire was transformational, enabling Alex and me to start focusing on getting product into stores. More recently, we hired our first Vice President of Marketing and Operations, as well as our first head of Sales. We aim to hire the best of the best, to help us promote the four core principles of who we are: food, sustainability, design, and education.

Dealing with competition presented us with a big learning curve; we've come up against copycats from around the world, including places as varied as South Africa and Taiwan. One of the competitors, funnily enough, boldly copied and translated our site word-for-word. But, at the end of the day, aside from trying to stay ahead of the curve by filing for patents and trademarks, we would rather spend $10,000 innovating and engaging our community than fighting legal battles. There are always going to be copycats, imitation being in some ways a sign of success. We don't want to build a company on the foundation of a legal fight.

Product development is our main focus. It took us two and a half years to go from the mushroom kit to the aquaponics kit; that was our MBA. We learned so much about business and what it takes to launch a product. Now, we want use what we learned to get amazing new products to our consumers faster, to keep them engaged and excited.

Chapter 7

Piquing Investor Interest

We're living in a defining era; in the mists of this global uncertainty lies inspiring opportunities for those who call themselves entrepreneurs. I've learned over the years that entrepreneurship is a craft, and as with any craft, it requires unwavering commitment, personal sacrifice, and above all, the resilience to bounce back. The best entrepreneurs understand that before commercializing any ideas, you must first get intimate with your customer. In *The Lean Startup*, Eric Ries emphasizes the critical importance of building a minimum viable product early and testing it often in the marketplace. Only when you get that real time pulse of your target customer, will you be able to gauge the viability of your idea.

In his 40 years as a celebrated entrepreneur, philanthropist and venture capitalist, Alan Hall's acid test in evaluating business plans always starts with the marketplace—"An idea is worth nothing until it has been commercialized and there are paying customers. Some ideas will be wildly profitable; others will be a failed dream. In the end, remarkable ideas lead to compelling products purchased by vast markets of enthusiastic buyer." Here's how Alan is helping the next generation of entrepreneurs.

Alan Hall

Grow America founder Alan Hall shares 40 years of entrepreneurial and investor experience. Grow America aligns the partners, mentors and capital that entrepreneurs need to create and grow successful companies.

We regularly tell entrepreneurs, "before you leave your day job, consider the great sacrifices you're going to make and the risks you're going to take. This is not an easy period." We want people to recognize it's going to take many, many years before you gain any wealth, if ever.

In addition, be prepared to make personal sacrifices and to put your life on hold if need be. In terms of personal sacrifice, I've been luckier than most. I have six children, all of whom are now married and happy. I've got 15 grandchildren. However, even for me the journey involved sacrificing family time. In both the initial failed ventures, and later the successful ones, I put in lots of hours. Though I tried to strike a balance, I still missed many ball games, dance and piano recitals. But, overall I've been fortunate; I've worked with many entrepreneurs whose kids don't know them and who are now on their fourth spouse, all because work came first.

Aside from recognizing the personal sacrifices involved, the unique thing successful entrepreneurs possess is the recognition that it's a journey, not a destination. It's something they're going to have to stick with. Many people just can't put in that kind of time, energy, and commitment. I was already 43 when I launched MarketStar, a global marketing solutions provider now part of Omnicom Group. Until then, I had experimented and failed five times. I had to go back to my day job after each failed attempt because I needed a salary to survive.

My partners and I have developed a process we use to help a thousand different companies a year. It is encoded in a template consisting of 32 questions pertaining to everything you can imagine in terms of running a business.

My background is marketing and sales, so I get excited about a business when I meet an entrepreneur who has nailed the needs of the customer, shown me a solution that addresses a rapidly growing market, and has relevant prior industry experience. When I see all that, I recognize the odds of success are going to be in our favor.

As an investor, I counsel entrepreneurs to engage customers early and often, making sure that each idea is really going to have commercial value. Earnings increase dramatically when people take that approach. The biggest reason why most entrepreneurs fail is they are sorely lacking in all the background information they need to be successful. To get at that information, they must answer the following questions: Why are the customers going to buy? How are they solving their problems right now? Am I the right person to take this product forward?

For example, if one comes up with an idea in the retail space, I'll ask, "Have you ever sold in retail? Have you ever worked at retail? Have you ever had any product sold through retail yourself?" If they answer, "No, but I do have a great retail product," I respond, You've got to have more than that; you need the network, the information, and the understanding of retail logistics to be successful."

Mentorship is really important in filling in the knowledge and industry expertise gaps. Find people in the industry in which you're going to be developing your business. If you have an idea for an outdoor sporting product, go find a mentor at an outdoor gear manufacturer. Make an appointment and say, "I need some help. Are you guys willing to spend a few hours helping me figure out how I can develop this? There might be a little financial reward for you as well."

When all is said and done, as an investor I've got to have early profitability; I've got to see that this thing breaks even and starts to make money quickly. I'm impatient about that. While I am patient about growth, recognizing that companies are going to take some time before they really accelerate and take off, I need to see that an entrepreneur can take an idea and quickly make it profitable.

The moment somebody actually has to put money down is the ultimate test of market viability. To that end, we have a program called AMP, Asking for Money for a Product from a focus group: Market research usually involves conditional statements like: "Would you buy this if…?". If people say, "Yes, of course I would buy," and then they don't, that's bad research. Our research model guards against this by asking people to give us a check for the product with the promise that we will return their money if it doesn't launch.

With respect to personal finances versus outside capital, I always tell entrepreneurs, "First, I want you to take your personal savings and sell your personal property, and invest the money in the business." I want to make sure you've got financial skin in the game, like I did, taking a second mortgage on my house when I started MarketStar.

Of course, you put in only so much. Once you've exhausted your own resources, turn to family and friends. To pitch them with high integrity, let them know they are investing in you more than your idea and stress that they may never get their money back. The next level, angel investors and venture capitalists, (people like me) who love to see a return. They want to be partners, right by your side. So now instead of being independent, you have a partnership. At some point, you establish relationships with banks: merchant accounts, some good savings accounts, credit cards. Finally, the time might come for an IPO, generating public funding.

Chapter 8

Discovering Your Customers' Needs

One of the pivotal points of my career took place in 1997 when I agreed to leave our Washington, DC operation to pursue an opportunity to enhance our firm's footprint in Central Florida. I had a young family, so I was naturally attracted to the climate and proximity to Disney World; still I was most eager to test my leadership skills with a talented group of young financial advisors whom I felt had a tremendous upside. Eager to have meaningful impact, I hired a prominent management consulting firm to help me evaluate the strategic direction of a region rich in opportunity, yet stuck in antiquated disciplines.

The process continued for six weeks, and while it unveiled a much more difficult challenge that I had originally anticipated, it reinforced Peter Drucker's mantra that, "the purpose of business is to create and keep a customer." As simple as that may sound, it was the wake call that we needed to truly understand that while many facets of our business were destined to change, the only constant would be our ability to know our customer, understand what she values, and consistently deliver it to her.

Obviously the landscape of business has changed since 1997, and as Brant Cooper and Patrick Vlaskovits describe in The Entrepreneur's Guide to Customer Development: A Cheat Sheet to The Four Steps to the

Epiphany, your thinking today should start by challenging your assumptions. Here's why.

Brant Cooper

The Entrepreneur's Guide to Customer Development co-author Brant Cooper discusses Customer Development, Minimum Viable Products, and the role of marketing.

Customer Development is a framework developed by serial entrepreneur Steve Blank exploring how successful companies developed, marketed, and sold their products. In our book, my co-author, Patrick Vlaskovits, build on Steve's foundation with a step-by-step methodology based on the following fundamental principles.

The first principle is that what you believe to be true about your business when you're first starting out is likely to be pure conjecture, business hypotheses. Though it's great that you believe in yourself and your idea, guesses are all you really have at this stage.

The second principle is that only customers hold the true answers. The way to validate your hypotheses is by asking your customers. It seems so incredibly obvious. However, CEOs, COOs, CMOs, and chief products people sit around and debate for hours the right move, marketing strategy, business model, or sales strategy. The most convincing person wins the argument and, often, that becomes the team's decision. The thought of actually engaging with existing or potential customers, to validate what is the right approach, rarely crosses the minds of many entrepreneurs.

So, here's the first step. Draw a picture of what you think your business model looks like given the ecosystem surrounding your business. What is your distribution method: retail stores or value added resellers? Do you think it's going to be the most attractive distribution method? Ask similar probing questions for other players such as partners, customers, and so on.

Next, ask, what is the value proposition your product brings to each one of those players? People often think of the value proposition in terms of their customer, but actually *any* participant in your ecosystem has a value proposition. If they're not getting value, they won't participate.

Third, ask: which of those players are mission critical to your business? If our value-added resellers went away, would that kill your business? Sometimes in a simple business you might have only your business. More commonly, though, business models depend on a complex distribution system.

Finally, identify the Minimum Viable Product (MVP): the minimum number of features you need in order to provide the value proposition for your mission critical ecosystem. This speeds up go-to-market and iteration. Entrepreneurs must guess at their minimum feature set, and it will probably fall short. Some mistakenly fear they have only one shot. They believe they're going to have tens of thousands of people trying their product, and if it does not have all the requisite features, they are nervous they will blow it. In reality, however, the number of users, and hence, the risk, is low. So, yes, while you are likely to fall short initially, it will be in front of a small and often forgiving audience.

You need to get your product or service out in front of the users as quickly as possible to validate that you're on the right path. One of the key things here is to unearth passion in your customer. Identify what they must have in order to become a lifelong customer. Shipping a finished product without having a relationship with your customer doesn't allow you to establish that.

Some mistake marketing for the Customer Development / MVP identification process. Getting the minimum viable product out the door is not the same as doing a marketing launch. It is not about doing a big public relations (PR) campaign. You're not running advertisements to test your minimum viable product concept. Instead, you're testing an actual product with a core constituency of early adopters in order to validate you have actually built the right solution.

Large consumer goods companies have done thorough Customer Development for a long time; they call it market research. Yet, somewhere along the way, market research for many startups came to mean: go find evidence that supports what you already believe. If you're taking your idea to an investor, convince that investor you have thought about all of these things and that a huge market does exist. So, you go to the trade magazines and you do some back of the napkin calculations, to find the evidence to support your hypothesis.

Steve Blank's Customer Development does not take that approach. Instead, it's trying to answer the question, if you were going work on this product for two years, spending all your time and money, wouldn't it be a good idea to figure out whether anybody actually wants it before you waste that time? That's really what Customer Development is: finding out if anybody actually has the problem you're trying to solve.

A key element of Customer Development is figuring out how to reach and convert your customers. When you get to that stage, it probably makes sense to bring on a marketing expert. I highly recommend, however, that this marketing expert is a doer, and not just a manager. You need someone who is actually going to be forming relationships with customers and validating the core business assumptions. That person needs to be heading the learning process; they have to be very hands on, and not just a people manager.

Chapter 9

Hooking Your Customers

Entrepreneurs see the world from a different vantage point; what appears obvious to them is likely invisible to most of us. The best ones are scanning the world each day to find routine problems that they can approach with fresh eyes—and when they do find one, their imagination takes over. They covet the experiment independent of the outcome, because for them, it's better to fail in originality than to succeed in imitation.

Yanik Silver is one such entrepreneur who's done it his way. Despite being on the forefront of the Internet marketing craze, he chose a different path from the beginning; a maverick approach to winning at a game that he created. Pay particular attention to his marketing philosophy.

Yanik Silver

Yanik Silver, author of the "Maverick" entrepreneur series, discusses some marketing hooks gleaned from an early start in sales.

To me, being a maverick is about changing the rules. So often, we business owners and entrepreneurs tend to focus on one thing: the bottom line. But my bottom line is triple: the maverick philosophy of make more money, have more fun, and give more. When we combine those, it gets really exciting.

My story starts with my dad. Our family emigrated from Russia when I was 2-½ years old in 1976, the U.S. bicentennial. My dad came here with $256 in his pocket. With no real command of the English language, he pretty quickly got fired from his job at the Washington Hospital Center and went to work for himself repairing medical equipment for doctors with private practices.

Growing up in a family business, I learned entrepreneurial lessons early which became embedded in me. I spent many summers working for my dad selling medical equipment, summers I didn't want to be working for him, when all my buddies seemed to be living at the beach. Yet, I came away with the philosophy of "sacrifice now for a better tomorrow."

When I turned 16, the deal was that I got a car if I went out and actually sold medical equipment. So, I was this 16-year-old punk, selling medical equipment door-to-door to 50-60 year old doctors; I grew up pretty quickly in the sales and marketing department (and I realized that cold calling was abysmal).

One of my clients, a doctor whose entire surgery center I outfitted, said, "You're into this marketing stuff a little bit, right?" I replied, "Yeah, sort of." He gave me a tape of an interview with Jay Abraham and Tony Robbins about optimization and direct response marketing. I thought it was fascinating that I could actually get paid just for writing something. That motivated me to learning all I possibly could on the subject.

I became, in essence, a copywriter because I was fascinated by the words that could actually get people to reach inside their wallets or get them to take action. So I began writing sales letters, and trying to share my method. I sold my method through direct response – writing a good sales letter to sell the sales letters. It sounds kind of funny in a way, but it had a really good hook to it (one of the five hooks I write about), the one I call "fish."

"Fish" has the basis in that old adage "If you give a man a fish, you feed him for a day, but if you teach a man to fish, you feed him for life." That very well may be, but the reality is people still want the fish handed to them. I believe the ideal is to teach people how to fish *and* hand them the fish at the same time, a pretty powerful combination. My particular fish products were fill-in-the-blank sales letter templates for just about any sort of business owner. That's what really took off.

The next level of products that really drive sales are the "silver platter fish." My first publishing foray was one step removed from what I was doing with medical doctors; I started consulting on the side for those who needed to attract patients seeking elective procedures. I decided to create a kit to help them do that, instead of trading my time for money: in fact, one of our big "Maverick" rules is, as much as possible try to avoid trading time for money.

So, I created a kit for $900. A bonus for buying this kit was what I called patient traction toolkits, based on a particular procedure, like liposuction, laser resurfacing, or breast augmentation. We had pre-done educational reports, postcards, press releases, letter locations, you name it. It was all in there. That was the driving bonus that got them to buy this $900 kit. That's where I learned about this idea of "silver platter fish" products that really drive sales.

Another hook is using specificity. The creator of 8-Minute Abs, a product which sold millions of copies, told me the name is what sold it. That's specificity: you only need 8 minutes a day to get six-pack abs. Similarly, a partner of mine and I created a product called 33 Days to Online Profits.

Yet another good hook is going the opposite direction of your competitors, if possible. In her great book, Different, Harvard Business School professor Youngme Moon talks about many businesses flailing because they don't have a distinct difference, or are merely trying to copy what their competitors already do well; this leads to a very average, middling kind of thing. Instead, show why there should be another product or service in your category; because if there is no reason for it, then you're just another Johnny-come-lately. Smart companies create distinctions and highlight them. For example, Mini Coopers have done a great job, playing up the car's small, quirky, funny nature.

But, even more importantly, Mini Coopers have not just highlighted a distinction, they have gone above and beyond by creating zealots, really passionate brand advocates. People that drive Mini Coopers are huge fans. It comes down to identity. Dead Heads, Trekkies, TED-sters, Parrotheads: all have a unique language to which like-minded people relate. In the same vein, I think "Maverick" is a word that resonates with entrepreneurs. Creating that unique language for a group creates identity.

Another way of creating identity is to engender the feeling of being part of something bigger than oneself. In Influence: the Psychology of Persuasion, Robert Cialdini argues that groups are more cohesive the more exclusive they are, for example high-end military groups like the Marines, Delta Force, Green Berets, or Navy Seals. But the stakes don't have to be quite this high in the business realm.

For instance, the Fiskateers is a really interesting group that was created for Fiskars, a consumer products company that makes, among other things, scrapbooking items, including scissors. The Fiskateers, a group of advocates for scrapbooking, don't let just anybody join. Those interested undergo a difficult process, having to prove their commitment to scrapbooking. That creates a community of zealots. Harley Davidson owners tattoo the logo on their biceps because they identify so strongly with Harley. Having their customers and fans rally behind them is what kept the company alive when they were going through some tough financial times.

In the long run, the goal is to create a bigger, more meaningful picture that will excite your customers, your fans. I think we all are looking for something we can latch onto that has a bigger purpose than just what we can achieve individually. Yes, one entrepreneur can change and transform an industry, but a thousand working together can change and impact the world. With the right group of people, you can influence the influencers and connect the connectors; you can leverage on a grand scale.

Chapter 10

Making Little Bets

What do Larry Page, Sergey Brin, Ed Catmull and Jack Dorsey have in common? While arguably amongst the greatest innovators of our time, they didn't begin with a brilliant idea—they discovered it.

In his latest book, Little Bets: How Breakthrough Ideas Emerge from Small Discoveries, Peter Sims inspires entrepreneurs to seek out interesting problems, ask a bunch of questions and prepare to be imperfect. When you decode the history of the valley's best success stories, it's clear that their greatness evolved over time. "Most entrepreneurs launch their companies without a brilliant idea and proceed to discover one, or if they do start with what they think is a superb idea, they quickly discover that it's flawed and then rapidly adapt."

Peter Sims

Little Bets author Peter Sims champions "design thinking," which leads to discovering the interesting problems.

I titled my book Little Bets to counter the tendency to think we need to have a big brilliant idea, a big bet. The reality is, from my perspective as a former venture capitalist, companies rarely start with a big, bold, brilliant idea.

More frequently, companies emerge the way Starbucks started: Howard Schultz had a vision of creating a coffee experience that was like the Italian coffee experience. But, the first stores in Seattle had non-stop opera music playing, menus written in Italian, and no chairs. As Schultz, one of the most effective entrepreneurs of his generation, has said, "We had to make a lot of mistakes." They had to discover what would eventually be thought of as a big, brilliant idea.

The same is true for Twitter, Google, and other companies we think of as icons. They don't begin with one big, brilliant idea. They begin with a lot of little affordable bets to discover what's going to work and what's not, through an iterative process. We never learn how to think like that in school. So, I felt that was an important message to convey.

Consider an analogy from the stand-up comedy world. Chris Rock is one of the funniest comedians in the business. But, to get there, he's gone through thousands and thousands of ideas, scribbled down on sheets of paper, worked out material in small comedy clubs, in front of small audiences, night after night after night – audiences of 40 to 50 people. Six months to a year later, he's got 60 minutes worth of rigorously tested material.

The same is true, I think, for companies that are starting out. Twitter began as a side project within podcasting company Odeo. One of the engineers at Odeo, Jack Dorsey, thought he could put together a short messaging technology that people would value. He tried that for two weeks and got enough people inside Odeo to think it was interesting, thus giving him another six months to work on it. After six months, enough excited people at Odeo were able to take it out more broadly. So, these small pilots, and testing and iterating and refining the idea, got them to South by Southwest, where Twitter really started to take off.

This mindset is very entrepreneurial, but it's also rooted in proven research. Design Thinking, a newly emerging field, teaches methods by which you can make these little bets successful. My book describes a number of surprisingly similar methods that span standup comedy, filmmaking, entrepreneurship, military counterinsurgency.

Making "little bets" means being comfortable with uncertainty. I've been trained as a very left-brained thinker. It's very counterintuitive for us who are trained in management thinking to try something without knowing whether it's going to work, to go through this iterative process to build up ideas, rather than being able to start with the answer.

The key is to first recognize that when you're in new territory, when you're in an extremely uncertain place, that's where these little bets and discovery skills come in very handy. When you know what you want to do, and you have a business that's going to be making 10 to 12 million dollars every year in a pretty predictable way, then you don't need to use methods of effective experimentation. You can just use the skills we've been taught through our schooling to solve those known problems.

But when you're faced with a situation where you're getting into a new market, or, for example, trying to build your personal network in a new area in which you really don't know the right influencers, you have to start small. Twitter is a great example of this. Anytime you follow someone on Twitter, you're making a little bet on that person, and you learn something from each of these little bets; it takes you more and more into a new area.

What the entrepreneurial CEOs like Amazon's Jeff Bezos understand is that you need to use many experiments to discover opportunities, and be willing to fail in the process. That's something that runs counter to the way we've been trained. Be willing to make errors, because it's the surprises that open up the cool opportunities. The key is to be willing to try. The research in psychology, including that of Dr. Carol Dweck, who is the leading expert on how people respond to failure and setbacks, shows that after you start, whatever you are doing becomes easier. Then you can develop what Dr. Dweck calls a "growth mindset," in which you are willing to be imperfect and realize that every small bet is an opportunity to learn, rather than something that's going to reflect poorly on you as a failure.

The most successful entrepreneurs think of learning the way most people think of failure. Dr. Saras Sarasvathy, at the Darden School at University of Virginia, researches and compares the way managers and entrepreneurs make decisions. She says that the key difference between the way managers think and the way entrepreneurs think is precisely what I saw when I was working with entrepreneurs and venture capitalists. Entrepreneurs aren't afraid of surprises, nor do they try to avoid them. They don't try to avoid errors, either, because they recognize that by taking a concrete action, they'll learn, whether it takes them down a path that's interesting or not.

The key insight is that, in the discovery phase, when you're in the unknown, you're trying to identify interesting problems -- whether it's a customer problem or need, or a joke idea that's going to light up the crowd for Chris Rock -- you're just trying to identify interesting problems. And once you find those problems, then you double down on them and make bigger bets as you go. But, in the case of the customer, that problem discovery phase really entails understanding customer needs, which often are unarticulated. People were not walking around saying, "I really want to have a Google search engine" before Google existed. So, you have to put it in front of them and see to what they respond well. That's one of the core elements of "design thinking" -- spending time understanding the customer's underlying needs.

The key initial stage in any venture is figuring out what problems should be solved. The cheaper and faster you can do that, the better. In this regard, the mantra is "failing quickly to learn faster" – start with the "minimum viable product," just start very small. With the Web, this has become a prevalent ideology around not just Silicon Valley but is also trickling out to other parts of the world very quickly.

Technology allows entrepreneurs to very, very quickly put things in front of people to see where the opportunities and problems lie. The cheaper you can do that without venture capital the better, because venture capitalists are going to want to see a business with billion-dollar potential. Venture capitalists have to have confidence that you're going towards really big problems.

At many business schools, when they talk about starting a venture, they say, "Do all the analyses, ascertain the market size, get every piece of information you can before you go out there and start talking to potential customers." Now, I do just the opposite; I go out and start talking with users until I figure out what the problems are and then build up to the analysis as I go.

Entrepreneurs work in an intuitive way without being trained. In fact, I think that's why Reid Hoffman, founder of LinkedIn, told me he has a problem with potential entrepreneurs who go to business school. He believes, as I do, that they have to unlearn a lot of what they've learned in business school to become successful entrepreneurs.

I had the opportunity to work with Chet Pipkin, founder of the Belkin Corporation, when I was working in venture capital at Summit Partners. Belkin makes products for your iPod; you probably have many of their products in your home and office.

When Pipkin started out, in his teens, he wanted to be an entrepreneur, but he didn't know anything. He just went out into the world and started observing, trying to find problems. He simply went down Hawthorne Avenue in Los Angeles during Christmas and said, "Should I start a Christmas tree service? A limousine service?" He eventually went to Radioshack and started observing what people were buying (this was the early 1980s, when the personal computer industry was starting to take off). People were buying printers, but they didn't have cables to connect them. So, Pipkin went out and made them, and that's how Belkin started.

The lesson is: you just need to ask the right questions to find interesting problems. The best entrepreneurs find their ideas by becoming immersed in the world. That's really how it works – you're constantly learning as you go. Having worked and studied with some of the leading entrepreneurs in the world, I can tell you they all ask questions voraciously – of me even. They all are voracious learners. So, for young people starting out, I'd suggest: ask lots and lots of questions, and just DO. Do things to discover what to do.

Chapter 11

Evolving a Startup

Starting a business is an invigorating experience, but rarely is it without challenge. As entrepreneurs, we're inspired by DOING, and for most of us, the legal stuff tends to bog us down; unfortunately, no business is immune to compliance. Corpnet co-founder and CEO, Nellie Akalp gives you the critical issues to watch.

Nellie Akalp

Nellie Akalp, founder and CEO of CorpNet.com, opens up about the journey of her startup from its first version to its current, second iteration.

In a nutshell, CorpNet.com offers document filing services to business owners seeking to incorporate, or if they're not ready to take that leap, to file as a sole proprietorship or partnership. We also provide various other services to existing business owners, such as trademark search registration services and compliance services. Our value proposition is that we take the hassle out of having to comb through a particular state's website to see what documents are needed.

For better or worse, there was actually no thought process behind our company's formation. I came home one hot summer day after working an 8-hour shift at a law office, with my pantyhose were torn, makeup running down my face, when I noticed my husband, sitting in our air-conditioned apartment surfing the Internet, and I thought, "If you don't get serious about finding a job, then there is no us."

That's when he said, "I have this great idea. It's called 'online incorporation. I know you don't know much about this. It's the birth of the Internet, but I just need a hundred dollars from you to buy a domain name. It's called MyCorporation.com. Sky Dayton (then, owner of EarthLink) is waiting for my answer."

After a couple of weeks, we put a one-page website up. There wasn't really much thought process put into it when we launched the website. Until now, I was supporting both of us while my husband was finishing law school. But, after we got our first client, we looked at each other and said, "Okay, it's time to get serious."

If it's not hard and if there is no risk, then it's really boring for us as serial entrepreneurs. My husband finally convinced me to quit my job. While he was studying for the bar exam, I transformed our two-bedroom apartment into a proper office and hired a couple of law clerks so they could assist me in processing the orders.

After putting up our one-page website, we got indexed in Yahoo and all the different viable search engines at the time. The first hundred days, I worked by myself, but once my husband finished the bar examination, as soon as he walked in the door, in fact, I said to him, "We need to add 'xyz' to our suite of services. We need to add rush services. We need to get a merchant service provider; boom, boom, boom, let's go for it." There was no methodology or business plan in place, whatsoever.

Now, the economic landscape is so different than it was then, at the birth of the Internet. Today's entrepreneurs definitely need some direction or business plan. I think for any small business owner, it's really important to have a roadmap in place, especially in a volatile or recessionary economic landscape.

I do not want to paint the picture that it's been perfect from day one with the launch of our second business, even with a business plan in place. We've had some struggles with CorpNet.com. We launched initially in 2009 with a business model that completely failed. We came out saying, "We've done this before, come on, we're going to do it again and we're going to be great at it." Of course, a couple of months into the business, we're looking around, wondering, "Okay, where are the phone calls? Where is the business?" and it became very clear to us that our pricing model was flawed.

As an entrepreneur, you have to have the stomach for change and you have to be very reactive. When we immediately implemented a price increase all across the border, we saw a substantial increase in sales, about 30%. We found that people wanted to do business with us, perceived the service as valuable, but were actually thrown off by why we charged so little. Our low price sent the wrong signal about quality; our price increase immediately increased sales.

I have a clear vision as to where I want my business to go and where I want to be in one year, two years, and five years, but I also have the stomach for change. I also have a sense of humility that I have gained in running my second business; it's essential to have other people come in and evaluate your business and tell you what you're doing well and what you're doing wrong. I've humbled myself to the point that I am listening to my colleagues and to my peer group in this regard.

Version 1 and Version 2 of CorpNet.com are as different as night and day. Yes, from the clients' perspective, we are still providing a one-stop shop for new and existing business owners who want to either start a business or maintain an existing business. The real change has happened *inside* the company. My husband, Phil, and I are much more engaged with the day-to-day aspects of the business.

In addition, with the second business, I'm much more involved on a macro level. Whereas, with the old version of the company, I was much more involved in the actual day-to-day of the business, now I'm the face of the company with respect to business development and new opportunities. I do all of the relationship marketing, all the social media, all the branding. Also, I am in charge of tracking the sources of traffic to our website. I'm very much involved in figuring out why we're making the profits that we're making today, or why we're not.

Section 2:
Pivot or Persevere

Chapter 12

Stacking the Odds in Your Favor

Dynamite author and entrepreneur, Carol Roth, shares her 'Simon Cowell meets Susie Orman' advice. "I wanted something that people were going to stop and say 'hmmm...this is really different and let me learn more.' The market place is very crowded for everything, including business advice. If I didn't capture their attention immediately, the chances that they were going to stop and learn more were slim to none."

Carol Roth

Former investment banker, media pundit, and author of <u>The Entrepreneur Equation</u>, *Carol Roth, opines on being realistic about the odds.*

I am trying to do my small part in increasing entrepreneurial success rates, so that entrepreneurship and small business can be the engine that drives growth in this nation. Because 90% of businesses fail, or fail to succeed in five years, millions of people are overwhelmed, overworked, and are making bad business decisions, ending up with things that look a lot more like jobs and a lot less like businesses. My framework does not rely on a certain number of steps to success; that doesn't work. We all have different definitions of what success is and we have different circumstances, goals and objectives. Moreover, those definitions change many times over the years as our circumstances change.

I wanted to enable anybody, whether just starting a business, stuck in an ongoing business endeavor, or just interested in the state of entrepreneurship, to have a framework that examines their motivation, time-horizon, opportunity, personality, and circumstances to evaluate whether the rewards greatly outweigh the risks. I prompt people to answer the following questions before they go into business: Have I done everything to stack the odds in my favor? Does this make sense for me? If not, what do I need to go do in order for this to be a better choice for me? When more people ask themselves these hard questions, those entrepreneurial success statistics can begin to change.

The path towards greater personal and professional fulfillment, especially as an entrepreneur, requires the willingness to be comfortable with being uncomfortable. I had to learn that myself first. I gravitated to things at which I excelled; I tended to avoid playing games I couldn't win. That did not serve me well, because not knowing how to fail, not knowing how to take on risks and learn from them and grow, was stifling my growth. Having the discomfort, the growing pains, catalyzes breakthroughs.

Ask yourself, "Am I willing to get comfortable with being uncomfortable, or do I just want to maintain the status quo?" If you're not willing to fail, and possibly fail big, to endure the rollercoaster, then it's not the right time and you should wait. Then keep revisiting your decision until it is the right time for you.

For example, there are times in my life where I put off what I'm doing today because, although financially viable, emotionally I couldn't commit. Growing up, I was taught we would be living in a box under Lower Wacker Drive if we didn't save every penny, an attitude towards finances I had to unlearn before I could take my own personal risks.

Having said that, I think many aspiring entrepreneurs dive in too quickly, underestimating what it takes to start a business and keep it going. One hears stories about people starting businesses for a hundred dollars, a thousand dollars, three cereal box tops, but that's really just a small piece of the puzzle. Not only do you need the capital to start a venture, but you also need to be able to operate it for at least a couple of years while you build a foundation. Nobody is sitting around waiting for your business to open, and there is no confetti that falls from the sky the day you cut the ribbon. Furthermore, you also need enough money to live on. Yes, it could cost you a hundred dollars to start, but that's just a fraction of the money you'll need to survive that initial phase.

In addition, I worry that younger entrepreneurs don't do enough to gain the experience that stacks the odds in their favor. What I hope is that those who have an entrepreneurial spirit will start at a younger age exploring what it means to run a business and getting a realistic perspective on what it takes, so that by the time they graduate they're in a better position than I was.

Ideally, young entrepreneurs should be in the position of my friend, fashion designer Jason Wu. Jason designed Michelle Obama's gowns for both inauguration ceremonies and is currently a darling of the New York fashion scene. When he had the opportunity to design Michelle Obama's first gown he was 26. Everyone exclaimed, "Oh my God! Who is this kid? He's an overnight success."

Well, Jason had been working in the industry since he was 16. He was the creative director of one of my clients at a very, very young age and then he interned for Narciso Rodriguez. So, it was an overnight success 10 years in the making. I think today's young entrepreneurs have the opportunity, with technology and all the information that's available to them, to gain experience at an early age.

Having experience is crucial because I am concerned that low entry barriers will entice young entrepreneurs to rush in without sufficient preparation; if you fail to prepare, you prepare to fail. The most successful entrepreneurs are the risk mitigators; they test out their ideas to gain relevant experience and stack the odds in their favor before they began. Certainly there is always a random success story that defies the norm; theoretically we can all be a ruler of an island nation or marry a supermodel, but very unlikely. I wouldn't bet my life savings on it.

I think you need to be comfortable with risk, but also be prepared and mitigate it; be strategic, but be willing to work day-to-day; be willing to ride that rollercoaster, but be able to stomach the high highs and the low lows. You have to be comfortable with change, you just need to get used to it.

Chapter 13

Having an "I'll Figure it Out" Attitude

While most fifteen year olds are cramming for a Spanish exam or rushing to soccer practice, Danny Iny was meeting with CEOs to build a game that would enhance the learning experience. Danny was a rare teen with a powerful vision and a high-level of courage. As he met with these high level executives, he pitched his idea with such zest that a stranger agreed to a partnership. Danny's ignorance fueled his creativity and relentlessness while building the learning game. Though his experiment ultimately failed, his learning was just beginning. Today, Danny is one of the most influential bloggers and Internet personalities; here's how he continues to engage his audience.

Danny Iny

Danny Iny, co-author of Engagement from Scratch!, relives his entrepreneurial journey from his teenage educational gaming years through building Firepole Marketing.

My story starts at age 15 and being really bored at school. After cutting classes for about a year and a half, I decided to make it official and quit school to start a business building websites. Why building websites? Because I knew some HTML and figured I could make it work. Of course, anyone reading this who knows HTML understands that logic doesn't mean anything; it's like saying "I know the alphabet so I should be able to be a successful author." Building a good website has less to do with the technology and more to do with understanding the aesthetics of creating the desired user experience. I didn't even know what all those concepts were at the time. But I dove in anyway.

One day, a friend of mine, his seven-year-old sister, and I were playing an educational videogame. I looked at the screen and said, "You know what, I think I could build something like this." Entrepreneurs accomplish a lot of what they do because they're too naïve to realize how unrealistic their ideas are. If you've got this big exciting goal and someone says it's not possible, then double-check your assumptions, but go do it anyway. You never know; you might surprise yourself and other people.

I found the game box, looked up the contact information, and called the company. Somehow, I got a meeting with the CEO. In hindsight I think, how the hell did I pull that off? At the time, though, it didn't even occur to me it was a big deal. So, I walked into the CEO's office. Remember, I'm 15. We sat down and I said, "I would like to propose a business relationship. I think I can build the games and you can sell them." My mom has a degree in psychology. So, naturally I tell him I've conferred with a psychologist and I've reached the conclusion that if you really want kids to learn, you have to make learning fun and make it something that happens in the background.

What this guy could have said was, "No kidding. I've been doing this for 10 years. Get out of my office." But instead, he opens up a drawer. He pulls out a document and blows on it, sending a cloud of dust flying. He says, "Look, this is a script I wrote for a game about eight years ago. Why don't you build it and we can chat." I reply, "No problem. That sounds great!"

The CEO added, "What are you going to build it in?" I responded, "Visual Basic." Not that I knew Visual Basic, but I had a friend who did, and I thought I could impose on him to teach me. The CEO said, "Isn't that like reinventing the wheel? Why don't you build it in Director?" I replied, "Look, if we're going to be doing business together, obviously, I have to adapt to your business practices. No problem. I'll do it in Director." We shook hands. When I got home, I Googled: "What is Director?"

Having a confident, "I'll figure it out" attitude is really important for an entrepreneur. Your job by definition is to create something new; there is no playbook. There are uncertainties. Of course, you want experience to mitigate some of that risk, and you do want to think through what you're doing, but there are things you don't know how to do and you have to trust you are able to figure them out when they come up. I worked on my first educational game for a long time. Though it never launched (mostly because I didn't know what I was doing), I learned a lot in the process.

Fast forward to a few years ago, while I was living in Montreal, I decided to build another educational game. I bootstrapped. People talk about "bootstrapping," but don't always understand what it really means. Many think it means doing things on the cheap. However, bootstrapping isn't only about money. Rather, it is about leveraging resources to do two things: first, to take the next step, and second, to expand the pool of what you have at your disposal in order to take more steps in the future.

I wanted to build a game, but what did I have in my early 20s? I had a little more experience than I did when I was 15. But I still didn't know all that much. I didn't have money. I didn't have much to work with. I did have commitment, drive, and relationships with people. So, I sat down, did some research, and wrote a design document. I showed the document to some friends and said, "I really want to build this and I think it's going to be amazing. Why don't you get involved and help me do it?"

They got behind it, investing some of their time and energy. One thing led to another, and eventually this turned into a pretty exciting startup called Maestro Reading. We were building software to teach kids how to read, something I was very passionate about.

The education space is a very complicated market. In hindsight, perhaps it was not the best place for a CEO in his early 20s. The content was great; the kids loved it, as did the experts. Unfortunately, the parents and teachers, for a variety of reasons, didn't really get it.

My five or so employees and I realized we had to pivot. We hit on a much better way of getting our stuff to the kids we wanted to reach, and wrote up a new business plan. We were all set, ready to make this change, and then the market crashed and there was just no more money. I had to let my employees go, many of whom were my friends. I got stuck with about a quarter of a million dollars of debt. There was only one thing we could do: rebuild.

I've learned much in my journey. One lesson is: recognize you're going to get a lot of things wrong. You're going to fall down and it's going to hurt, but that's okay. I think Eric Ries says that if you want to be a successful entrepreneur, try to fail quickly so you can get it out of the way, learn your lessons, and keep on going. In fact, an investor I know will not put money into a business in which the founder has known only success, because failure will come sooner or later.

Failures are not bad as long as you learn. Think of starting a business like being in a relationship. Your first or second relationship doesn't work out, but you learn something each time. Then when you meet the right person, when you're ready to make that commitment and start a life together, the lessons you learned from those previous relationships are part of what allow you to make it work with the right person. That doesn't mean those break ups didn't hurt. It doesn't mean you don't need some time to recover. But, eventually, you lick your wounds, you pick yourself back up, and you get out there again.

A guy I used to work with liked to say: what I like about being an entrepreneur is that if you take away everything I've got and I have to start from scratch, give me a week and I'll make money. Because being an entrepreneur is about looking around, seeing opportunities, and finding ways to fill those needs.

Chapter 14

Thriving

We are still living in a male dominated corporate hierarchy. According to this year's Fortune 500, only 18 firms are led by female CEOs and one in 10 of those firms still have no women on their boards. The good news though is that women today own nearly 50% of all businesses in the US, and that number continues to rise.

There are many reasons on why women thrive in business, but it's their adaptability, networking capabilities, and empathy that make them stand out. Nada Jones is convinced that each woman something powerful to contribute to the world. She has created the platform *ltd365.com* to help women realize their dreams. She believes that the journey begins when you crystallize your purpose and continues only through action. Here's how she's directing her entrepreneurial life.

Nada Jones

Nada Jones, creator of ltd365.com, ltdLIVE, and ltd Magazine (ltdMAG), and author of <u>16 Weeks to Your Dream Business</u>, inspires women to pursue their entrepreneurial dreams by figuring out how to "thrive" (vs. "balance") and heed (some) naysayers.

Amazing women entrepreneurs believe they're here on this earth to do something only they can do. They've taken their vision and put it into action. These women inspire me the most.

For those women who want to pursue something outside the home, entrepreneurship offers the financial opportunity, to some extent, to choose and control their life and career. People often ask why I became an entrepreneur. I reply that I couldn't find a job description for what I wanted to do, so I created my own, a common refrain among people who know they have something unique to offer.

I tell the women who come to me (and for obvious reasons they're coming to me because they're longing for something else): "You're missing out on an opportunity to pursue your passion; you're missing out on an opportunity to create extra income. That income may allow you a few more vacations. It may allow you to put your children through college. It may allow you to even get the house you want, to travel as you want."

Women working in a traditional setting complain of lack of job security. They say, "I'm working hard and I'm building towards somebody else's future, not my own. I'm helping somebody else get rich. I'm not doing the thing I'm fully capable of because my job is limited to my job description." They're also surely missing out on flexibility; what I hear most often is the "9-to-5 thing" is not working for them or for their families.

Of course, being an entrepreneur is daunting. And it can be daunting for different reasons for different women. When I started my own business, failure scared me the most. Money wasn't the issue; rather, it was the question: "Can I really achieve my vision, can I make what I'm so passionate about work?" On the other hand, for some women the consideration is primarily financial. And for still others it's, "If I'm doing this for flexibility, and it ends up sucking all my time, then I'm just not where I want to be."

When a woman with a family, like me, becomes an entrepreneur, her role as a mother and a wife does change. I once interviewed moms about work-life "balance" and I realized everybody defined it differently. In fact, some people just didn't believe it existed, so they questioned why we were having a conversation about it at all. And even if you buy into the idea of "balance," when you try to balance commitment to family, to business, to being a wife or a life partner, you have to add little weights to make sure that everything is in constant balance, and then you become a slave to the balancing process itself.

Instead, think of "thriving" as superior to "balance." For me, thriving means I can prioritize the top three things my children need from me, my husband needs from me, my house needs from me, my business needs from me, and my friendships need from me, and act accordingly. What can I cut away? Maybe this isn't a season for certain relationships. Maybe it's not the time for me to be on the parent association at the school, so I'm going to minimize my time to only a few hours. Or maybe, I'm not going to every single practice, but I am going to go to every game.

Having the time to be all things to all people and be everywhere at the same time is impossible. You will run yourself ragged and you'll be useless for everyone, including yourself. I don't believe it's really about making sure that everything is evenly checked across the board at all times. I think it's about looking at your particular season, situation, and family dynamic and figuring out what it is going to take to have that working optimally. You'll be surprised: it takes a lot less than you think. It just takes focus, and it doesn't take a lot of time to get focused.

Women entrepreneurs also have to deal with naysayers. Most painfully, they're even in our families. However, don't disregard them all. Some naysayers actually have something to offer. But, just like everything in life, be strategic in whom you listen to and whom you do not.

If you want to remove a blueberry stain from your child's shirt, you're not going to talk to people who don't know anything about stain removal. If you want to discuss an addition to your home, you're not going to talk to a neighbor who knows nothing about additions. Go to the people who have influence and expertise in the specific area you're pursuing. Pay attention when these experienced people throw you a curve ball or ask a question you can't answer, or look at you with the face that says: "I'm not sure if this is going to work or I'm not sure that you've crossed all of your T's and dotted all of your I's."

In my own experience, having a more critical outside eye with respect to my company's social media practices would have been extremely helpful. On one hand, we got the big picture right. When I look back at my first year of my business, ltd, (rather than my first year as an entrepreneur), what we did right was to launch our event ltdLIVE first. We "nailed it" from a branding point of view, because we really understood who our audience was and what she wanted. She wanted something that looked like her people coming to our conference: from collateral material looking pretty, to the setting looking sophisticated, to the speakers in the panel being women of note who can offer sound, inspirational advice. We understood our audience, we got the brand right, and we worked tirelessly on the details.

On the other hand, what we didn't get right, and we're still working on, is the social media component. Although I understood that social media had a place, I didn't really understand how important it was. We had a

Twitter and a Facebook account, and were blogging occasionally, but I wasn't doing it every day like I should have been.

Chapter 15

Cultivating Serendipity

Growing up in Washington, DC, I had great admiration for the vibe of Silicon Valley. From a distance, it was impossible to gauge the essential ingredients that make the Valley such a rich ecosystem, but even to an outsider, it was clear that its environment was the big differentiator. People in the Valley simply behave differently; they have an unwavering belief that the future will be vastly different from the present; they embrace loyalty and reciprocity as a way of life; and perhaps most importantly, they understand that relationships and reputations are the hallmarks of any successful endeavor. As an executive and an entrepreneur, I work hard to embody that mindset and to continually learn new ways to build such an inspiring environment.

Venture Capitalist, Victor Hwang wrote The Rainforest to give us a glimpse of what makes Silicon Valley tick. In it, he uses the natural Rainforest metaphor to propose that when a community operates like a rainforest "not controlling the specific processes, but instead helping to set the right environmental variables," it will likely foster the social behaviors necessary to maximize the "free flow of talent, ideas, and capital in a human network." Here's how the rules of The Rainforest, can help improve your odds of success.

Victor W. Hwang

Victor Hwang, author of The Rainforest Blueprint, *explains Silicon Valley's "rainforest" ecosystem.*

Most people, when they think of Silicon Valley, think of a place. They think of institutions: Stanford, venture capital, successful companies.

But what people in Silicon Valley system know is that it's not a place, it's a mindset. Silicon Valley is a particular set of assumptions about how you interact with others. Most people, even when they visit, don't identify it immediately; you've got to look under the rocks a little bit. And when you see it, you will find an unwritten, unspoken social contract.

One component of the social contract is the idea that you pay it forward; more often than not, people will help new entrepreneurs. They'll introduce you to someone. They'll give you a free piece of insight. They'll send you a news article. They'll give you some strategy from their own experiences. You take this behavior for granted when you're in Silicon Valley.

In other parts of the United States and of the world, people tend to help only those they already know, coming through for their own family or friends; they don't help strangers. In Silicon Valley, people help strangers. That approach sounds simple, but it's so powerful if you think about how it affects an entire community.

The reason we called Silicon Valley "The Rainforest" is because a rainforest is a highly serendipitous environment, unlike a highly controlled environment such as a farm. What's uncontrolled tends to become most valuable. For example, if you think of some of the great companies in Silicon Valley, you think of Facebook. Eight years ago, Facebook was this thing no one really predicted, something that on a farm might be considered a weed. Well, it turns out the weeds, those things that look like the opposite of what you're trying to grow, often become the 'Facebooks' of the next generation.

If the trick is cultivating these random environments, then the question becomes how do you plant rainforests and how do you grow them? We set out to describe how to build environments of randomness that are highly productive.

There are many definitions of success. On Wall Street, in investment banking, the definition of success is very predictable and measurable. It's money you create, deals you've closed, and that's fine. It works very well for that kind of ecosystem.

But what is success in innovative ecosystems like Silicon Valley? Folks like Mark Zuckerberg and Steve Jobs did not principally set out to make money; for them, it was the joy of creation, the joy of expression, the joy of building something.

I think for many entrepreneurs, the definition of success is very personal. When the definition of success is yours and not someone else's, then you are properly motivated. When you choose the journey, you enjoy the process a lot more, and no matter how hard it is, you tend to stick with it. If it's someone else's definition of success, people tend to quit early.

Innovation is not synonymous with production. Production is scaling something up that you know people want, like the iPhone produced by

Foxconn in China. But the innovation lies in the process of creating the next generation product and designing the software interface.

What's interesting about innovation versus production is that the cultural mindsets are different. In an innovative community, you look for randomness, for unpredictability. You look for many ideas generated very, very quickly in a community where people are tolerant of mistakes. Conversely, in production, you don't want any mistakes; you want fixed signals, predictability, and control.

In Silicon Valley, it's really about figuring out how to move from chaos to control, and doing it over and over again. It's that journey of going from a highly random system to a highly controlled system, and building very successful companies out of that, that is really the magic of these places.

The very first step in the "rainforest blueprint" is to get yourself together. If you have a bunch of hang-ups and insecurities, they're all going to come out at the worst times, alienating the people around you. This is especially so in high energy businesses where everyone knows the boss' hang-ups. Insecurities spread and grow in high stress situations. Getting a grip on yourself is absolutely critical, because it keeps the team you're building together in the worst of times.

Assembling your own kitchen cabinet, the advisors and mentors, to help you modulate some of your worst insecurities is also essential. Even incorporating things like meditation and yoga are extremely helpful in this initial phase of the blueprint. For example, one of the things we do in our workshop on building innovative communities, our "rainforest architect program," is meditation. We meditate in a natural ecosystem, a natural rainforest, not for very long, but long enough to understand you have to get comfortable with yourself if you're trying to do innovative work.

Decision making processes are also absolutely crucial. This is something more established businesses often forget because they think "content is content." However, innovative teams of small groups of people know "context is content" – how you shape the conversation affects the quality of the output of the conversation.

Do you always have your meetings in the same old boring conference room and expect a different outcome? Do you hold meetings in a lively place that's brightly lit and makes people happy? What's your meeting setup? Is attending meetings drudgery or do employees feel like there is something interesting to be discussed? Making small changes in how meetings are setup and the process by which interactions are created, actually drive their success. We know this is true at an intuitive level, but often forget it in day-to-day life.

In cultivating the rainforest, cognitive behavioral therapy also plays a part. This branch of psychiatry posits that people change behavior by changing activities. When you try out different options, you realize there are better ways to do things. With that in mind, if you're trying to build a community, an ecosystem, think about how you can give people real stuff to do. So, instead of just telling them to work in diverse innovative teams, help set up those teams for them. Then, the interaction with diversity will cause them to say "Aha, I see it. I actually understand it now more than I would have if you told me." If you put me on a small team that is designing an interesting product, I'll learn a lot faster than by reading some theoretical dissertation about it.

Finally, nourishing the rainforest involves the "rainforest scorecard." No one has really been able to measure these innovative ecosystems very effectively, so we decided to create our own measurement system. Our "rainforest scorecard" does not take the usual approach of looking at either economic systems or business systems, which are focused on cash-in/cash-out, salaries, jobs, hard metrics. Instead, we've tried to measure the "soft stuff."

Once you start an enterprise, you can't change something unless you can measure it, even the soft stuff. To that end, we score things like leadership, trust, role models, culture, patterns of behavior that are typically hard to assess. Our website allows entire communities to start to measure their rainforest together. One hundred people in a company can go online to this rainforest scorecard and create an aggregate score for the whole ecosystem there.

In nourishing the rainforest, keep in mind that failure is also a type of learning; something didn't work, and now you're a little wiser for it. The goal is not to make any failure too painful. Obviously, failing big could be the end of your company. So, ideally set up experiments where failure is okay. You're going to have many failures before you have success. The goal is to fail inexpensively and quickly.

Failure is really just a way of trying something and learning from experience. Again, going back to my initial point, if you have insecurities and hang-ups, failure can be catastrophic, a lot more catastrophic than it needs to be. But, if you're pretty self-assured and you understand the process you're going through, then failure is just a way of learning.

Chapter 16

Driving Startup Success

Look closely at a successful technology startup, and you're likely to see a founding team that includes a hacker, a hustler and an artist. The hacker builds the engine and makes it run seamlessly; the hustler is on mission to build brand awareness and bring in revenue; and the artist is relentlessly working to create an amazing user experience. This strategy is the modern equivalent of the assembly line and is part of The Startup Owner's Manual that the brilliant duo of Steve Blank and Bob Dorf continue to promote. This is the path of Silicon Valley and here's why it will dramatically improve your odds of success.

Bob Dorf

The Startup Owner's Manual co-author, and serial entrepreneur, Bob Dorf champions a passionately-led, customer-driven business model.

When I look back on both my successes and my failures, I see that I've learned four lessons concerning people, product, getting past break-even, and knowing when to pivot.

The number one lesson is that successful ventures hinge on people who are driven. They may not be necessarily the very best at what they do, but they have a passion to do great things. Let me illustrate. Back in 1972, at the age of 22, I quit a spectacular job that paid $250K (in today's dollars) to start Bob Dorf Communications. When we were up to about 50 or 60 people, we had a management retreat. In one particular 90-minute session, we talked about what makes a good Bob Dorf Communications person. We had all these wordy flip charts. Finally, Dorothy Crenshaw spoke up and said: "What makes people great here is not any one of these things, it's four words: fire in the belly." Driven, passionate people compensate for weaknesses by working harder or smarter, getting the help they need from others.

A trifecta needs to lead these passionate people -- a hacker, a hustler, and an artist. This was not a particularly ingenious concept by my co-author, Steve Blank, and me; nonetheless, it's becoming a mantra in Silicon Valley. The hacker is the brilliant, product-facing developer or engineer. The hustler is the customer-facing leader of sales, marketing, and customer development. The third member of the team, the artist, is charged with figuring out how to craft customer feedback into something that is easy to use, attractive, intriguing, and provocative. On the other hand, a one dimensional team, especially one exclusively made up of hackers, is almost guaranteed to fail.

The second big lesson I learned is about finding product/market fit. I saw that very clearly in my sixth start-up, Marketing 1to1. We hit a point when we suddenly figured out exactly what it was we were really great at:

driving comprehensive CRM strategy and implementation. Once we figured out the kinds of companies that were enthusiastically interested in that offering, we went from a pond of new business opportunities to an ocean of them. The sad thing is that more than three quarters of the start-ups I meet are still struggling to find that magic through internal consensus. Their problem is not knowing that not all votes matter; the only ones that do count are the customers' votes.

To achieve product/market fit, get out of the building to test, refine, and iterate your answers to the following questions in parallel with your product development effort:

- Who are your customers?
- What do your customers want to buy from you?
- How do they want to buy it?
- How are you going to find customers?
- How are you going to price the product?

We like to challenge start-ups to think about the 10 or 15 or 50 people who will be the most excited to adopt your product and to provide feedback on how to make it better. Nobody gets it right on the first time or the fifth time or the twelfth time. Too many start-ups overlook the vital importance of that kind of ignition that is the fastest, and perhaps only, route to start-up success.

The biggest mistake entrepreneurs make when they do get out of the building is pitching their product right away. They think, "I'm an entrepreneur. I'm supposed to sell. I'm supposed to make stuff happen." So, they go right to, "Hey, look at my really cool prototype. Isn't this great?

Wouldn't you like to buy one?" That cuts off all of the feedback they need to get in a much more fluid kind of environment.

The first time entrepreneurs get out of the building, they should not talk about the product at all. Instead, they should talk about the problem they believe their product will solve or the need they think their product will fill. This is a discovery process, not a sales pitch, aimed at understanding the magnitude of the problem and the size of the market which will gain them the knowledge and earn them the right to pitch.

A great example of this is a Bogotá-based team we worked with that was building an e-commerce art gallery. Though not a brand-new idea, this one had a few novel twists. One afternoon, they went to three art galleries. In the first one they said, "Hi, can we see the manager? We're thinking about selling your art on the Internet." The manager replied, "Thanks. I'm not interested. Have a nice day." The second gallery conversation went much the same way and produced very little feedback.

In the third gallery, the team looked around for a little while. They waited until the owner got up from her chair, came over, and started talking. For the first few minutes, they talked only about art, expressing curiosity about a lithograph on the wall. Then, when the owner was starting to think maybe she had a customer on the line, they said, "We're really not here to buy. We're here thinking about how to take some of this great art and sell it online."

They talked to that gallery owner for three-and-a-half hours about what works and what doesn't. The conversation went on at length in a very casual, gentle way because the owner was curious. She was looking for new ways to reach customers and new ways to sell. The team got all kinds of feedback on who the art buyers are, how to find them online, how prior ecommerce art galleries failed, and so on. At the end of the conversation, they shook hands and the gallery owner said, "As soon as you're ready, I'm willing to be one of your first customers."

Lesson number three, connected to the first two, is: life gets more exciting when you can get your idea to break even. You are able to take a deep breath and make decisions more strategically about what you're doing, how you're selling it, and how you're delivering it. Once you are past the ticking time bomb of a zero bank balance, you can truly focus on the best interests of your customers and employees.

Finally, the fourth lesson has to do with when to pivot and when to persevere. A pivot is a major change in one of the key components of your business strategy. For example, going from a paid website to a free ad-supported website, or going from selling the product to leasing or renting it, or going from web marketing to television advertising to acquire customers are all dramatic changes in a key element of your business and not to be taken lightly.

Chapter 17

Fighting Fear

"The core message of *The Art of Non-Conformity* is that you don't have to live a life that other people expect you too. And you can do good things for yourself and for others at the same time." Chris Guillebeau shares the core message of the book.

Chris Guillebeau

The Art of Non-Conformity author, and globe-hopping traveler, Chris Guillebeau talks about finding fellow passionate people around the world, face-to-face and online.

The core message of Art of Non-Conformity is you don't have to live your life the way other people expect you to. You can do good things for yourself and serve others at the same time. It's not a dichotomy, it's an 'and' not an 'or.'

While remaining self-employed and travelling non-stop for more than a decade to over 150 countries, the most important lesson I have learned: I wish I had started sooner and not been afraid of change. For a long time, even in the midst of this process, I lived in fear of change, of doing things differently, of what people would think about me, of setting a big goal and then failing. I was even a little bit afraid of success as well, and what comes along with it. The more I've traveled this road, the more fulfilling and meaningful it's been. The more I followed my passion and tried to connect that passion with those of other people's, the more good things have transpired.

My own entrepreneurial journey was extremely organic, not strategic at all. As a 20 year-old, I wasn't a very good employee; I didn't want to have a boss. My primary motivation was to not have a day job. I wanted to do anything legally and morally to support myself without working for someone else. So, I started selling things on eBay, a relatively new website at the time. I learned website design, affiliate marketing, and Google AdWords, among other things.

For 5 to 7 years, it was all a bit random. Part of that time, my wife and I were living in West Africa, volunteering for a medical charity. After 9/11, like many people we were depressed, trying to figure out our place in the world, and wondering how to help others. I read of the civil war and the desperation in Sierra Leone, the poorest country in the world at the time according to the United Nations. But I also heard some positive stories about organizations, charities, and businesses that were making a difference there and I wanted to be a part of that.

The single individual who most inspired my wife and me to live in Sierra Leone was Dr. Gary Parker, a California surgeon who moved to West Africa. I read about how he left his American life behind, met his wife, a fellow volunteer, in West Africa and how they stayed for more than two decades, raising two children there. I found myself very challenged by his story. I kept thinking, if this guy can give up so much, so much more than I could, surely I can do something. Taking the plunge to work in Sierra

Leone was challenging, but also amazing and transformative, definitely the best decision we ever made.

To do it, I structured my life in a way that would allow my wife and me to live there for years. I did the business work at night, to pay the bills and enable us to volunteer. I became more strategic around 2007-2008, when we moved back to the United States. In graduate school, I began thinking about creating The Art of Non-Conformity project.

I've created a number of different online properties that provide income, allowing me to write, travel, and do what I want. Entrepreneurially, it's been a 10-year journey with some high points, but also its fair share of low points. One noteworthy low was my experience with a U.S. fulfillment house that was shipping things out for me while I was overseas. For about three weeks I had almost no communication from them. When I began to figure out what was going on, I received an email saying not only had they gone out of business, but they also hadn't been shipping any product for the previous two to three weeks.

I was faced with a disaster. Many of their customers were upset, of course, but most of them were based in the States, and many of those figured out another way to do things. I, on the other hand, was in Africa and trying to figure out a solution while simultaneously working full time for the medical charity during the day. That was definitely a low point.

Yet, that extremely challenging situation came with a silver lining: figuring out a solution and bouncing back. I thought, "I'm going to find a way out of this. I'm going to find a way to ship product, get some new printing done, find a new fulfillment house, and it's going to be okay. If I can get through this, then I can probably get through anything." Long story short, I sorted out the problem; it wasn't great, but it worked out. I look back on that as a turning point: we made it through a hardship without the business going bankrupt.

As I mentioned before, fear affects my decision-making, as it does for many. From time to time, I hear about the idea of "fearlessness," but I don't think that's realistic for most people, myself included. The way I learned to overcome fear was not to pretend it didn't exist, but rather to acknowledge it and say, "I do have fears, but I'm not going to let fear make my decisions for me." I know I want to make this product, become an entrepreneur, live in Africa, start a writing project, write a book.

Whatever it is I really want to do, fear will not dictate my decisions because I have enough experience now to know I'm going to regret it if I don't try. If I go out there and fail, sure that will sting, but it's going to be worse if I have the opportunity to do something and don't do it because of anxiety about the outcome.

I've always been an introverted, very shy person. In some of my past travels, for example to Asia or Latin America, where I didn't speak the language, several days in a row might pass before I speak to anyone. I'm still fairly introverted, but I've been encouraged and inspired by everyone who has connected with the Art of Non-Conformity project. I started doing meet-ups a couple of years ago at every city I go, hearing many stories about the kind of projects and dreams people are pursuing and what they hope to do with their lives. I've really been surprised in a pleasant way by how much fun, and how inspiring it is to connect with the right people.

As I mentioned, I have visited 150 countries so far, and have had a range of different experiences. Getting back to the idea of community, almost anywhere in the world now I'm connected with people through Twitter or through my blog somehow. Sometimes when I go to unfamiliar places, I will reach out through Twitter or the blog, inevitably getting responses from people who offer to host me and take me around. Apprehension about strangers notwithstanding, every time I've accepted the offer, it's always been a very positive experience, much more edifying than without a native guide.

With that in mind, the first step in expanding a community through social media is to put forward a message and to invite people to join it; to say, here is how I see the world and here is what I'm up to. If you're interested in this, then I would love to have you be a part of it, of what I call "a small army of remarkable people." Then, be accessible and be helpful to that small army. Respond to people on Twitter. Don't outsource your email, delegating that to someone else. If you're really in the business of building relationships, the business I'm in, the best thing you can do is to be genuinely helpful and take an interest in what other people are doing.

For aspiring bloggers out there who want to not only share their view with the world but also to make a living out of it, reverse engineer what other people have done; read widely and see how other people have done it. And then, as you go forward, align your passion with that of others. In other words, of the things that excite you, and at which you are skilled, what do you want to blog about that will also be interesting to someone else? Aside from friends and family, why should anyone else read your blog and why should anyone else care? The more you focus on meeting a need, providing a solution to a problem, or alleviating a pain point, the more successful you will be.

Chapter 18

Living Fearlessly

I've always felt that sport offers a great metaphor for entrepreneurship. Like the premier athletes, an entrepreneur has to have a deep belief in his ability, the humility to always put the team's interests ahead of his, and perhaps more importantly, the mind power to learn as much from losing as he does from winning. Reaching sport's top pyramid is a grueling ride, but for the few who get there, it's a portrait of their character.

Jude Gomila isn't your typical Internet entrepreneur; he's a visionary with a purpose to help you 'engineer your dreams.' He co-founded the gaming platform Heyzap because he's driven to build amazing products. Five minutes into my conversation with him, I was blown away by his ability to see a world that most of us miss. Here's what I mean.

Jude Gomila

Jude Gomila, co-founder of social gaming company Heyzap, shares how he faces the unknown.

The number of unexpected turns in the Heyzap journey has been most interesting. At every single juncture of building the company, we had no idea what would happen next. We had no idea that we would get Ashton Kutcher as an investor. We had no idea that we were going to get Union Square Ventures to be our backers. We had no idea at any time whether we were going to completely fail or build one of the greatest companies in the gaming industry. We still don't know.

Heyzap recently has expanded its user base. We now have around 10 million installs of the application – a very vibrant community of followers discovering what others are playing, comparing scores, getting achievements, etc. Since 2010, Heyzap has gone from being web-focused to being very mobile focused. Right now, we're building the community of game developers and letting them join the platform.

One way of handling the unknown is to be content with having nothing, knowing you may completely fail, run out of money, rack up credit card debt, and have to live a very frugal life. If that doesn't stress you out, if you'd be happy to try again, if you're content with being frugal, then I think you don't have anything to fear. Even if you lose everything you have, as long as you don't lose your friends, principles, and values, then you're just living a frugal life and you shouldn't need any more than that.

I have no fear of crashing. I don't mind if I fail, because I'll just go again. Maybe that is the biggest difference between people that build companies and people that are scared of building them. That resilience is partly due to my upbringing. As a college student, I had to be relatively frugal. After graduating, when I was building my first company, I had to be very, very frugal. This taught me how to be extremely effective with money and time, and I realized it didn't matter that I didn't have very much to go on because I was constantly learning new things.

The most challenging part of the Heyzap journey was at the start, and that's where being comfortable with frugality paid off the most. We had been involved with Y Combinator, raising around $30,000. We spent a lot of that money on our visas and our flights to get back to the United Kingdom because we were only allowed in the United States for three months at a time. When we started with Y Combinator, we actually had already burned through the original capital. We had to survive with basically zero money, going into credit card debt. We were going deeper and deeper into a black hole of debt and having to become more and more frugal, but at the same time we had to push ourselves further and further and take more and more risk to try to build the company.

Some people believe in going all out to expand rapidly, whereas I think it's better to be frugal with financing, too, because it is good training for how to be efficient. Most of the time, that initial $1 million is spent mostly on people or infrastructure. But, it's really about how *not* to spend the money.

When we first started Heyzap, my knowledge was theoretical. I knew economics, to a certain extent, as well as managerial accounting. Having studied engineering, I knew a fair bit about that, too. I knew products. When I was a kid I was always obsessed with products, taking them apart, putting them back together to fix them. I learned design at university, as well, and that became very important to me. Through Heyzap users, I've been learning more about design in a much more rigorous and practical way.

At least initially, I did not know enough about practical matters. I didn't know how to recruit people or how to build teams. I'm definitely learning more about people. That's the thing a university doesn't teach you -- how to find the right people and then get them to perform. In a university, you can learn all the theoretical things. You can even learn about how to build new products. But, it's very hard to learn how to put great teams together and to build culture before you actually run a business. One thing I learned about getting people to perform is that you should always hire those who share the vision of the company. A person might be the best engineer in the world, but if they don't buy into what you're making, then it's not going to work out.

We design our learning principles to stand the test of time; we try to abstract these into generalities (though sometimes we break the rules). Our book budget is used by engineers and sales people to buy books across any subject, not necessarily in their own field. We encourage everybody to learn then teach each other new skills, to be generalists, but also to refine the special skills they have – to get really, really good at their one or two special skills.

Chapter 19

Taking a Few Turns

Iteration reminds me of companies like Basecamp and Twitter; they ran with the fact that you don't always get things right the first time—the same way authors write drafts and athletes train. I especially like the idea of iteration because it takes the pressure off a bit. Instead of focusing on everything being perfect, you're expecting to make mistakes while preparing for reflection and reaction. You'll be able to fix the mistakes and improve your business with small steps, always making adjustments along the way. The most important thing to do is simply keep at it, and Immad Akhund, co-founder of Heyzap demonstrates why he's a living testament to the attitude.

Immad Akhund

Immad Akhund, co-founder of mobile gaming firm Heyzap, shares his startup's journey from formation to early traction as the company built strong internal and external relationships.

Heyzap is a mobile app for gamers on Android and iOS that allows people to discover games and see which ones their friends are playing. For developers to integrate with, we also have leaderboards for storing high scores online and an advertising network.

There was another company, OpenFeint, which had been doing leaderboards for quite a while. Initially, we chose to avoid that feature because they had significant market share. But in December 2012, OpenFeint shut down their leaderboards, so we stepped in. It fit fairly well with what we were doing because we already had a software development kit (SDK) for gaming and we already had a lot of gamers on our platform. We re-envisaged the way leaderboards work by making it much more social. A lot of leaderboards for mobile games had been anonymous. We required users to have a real identity with a real picture.

Mobile advertising is another interesting space, still in its infancy. We're still learning, but we think we have a pretty unique angle. Game developers are artists who want a very clean ad experience. From a gamer perspective, it's always good to have very relevant ads. We deliver ads inside of side-scrolling games (where onscreen characters run, jump, and climb to meet an objective) that look good and don't feel "spammy."

This is my third startup. After seven years, it feels good to get to a position where I think it can be a long-term independent company. There is something called "impostor syndrome," where you don't know whether you're doing something for sure or whether you're faking it. This is a dreaded feeling almost every entrepreneur has when they are first starting out. It's nice to be over that.

Of course, Heyzap has definitely taken a few turns. We initially started distributing Flash-based games on the web. Our current iteration has only been since 2011. I always think of startups as a journey of ups and downs. In the first few months after our launch, we exploded. It felt like we had hit on something that was going to grow forever. Over time things changed and we found it hard to bring in revenue.

As Rei Inamoto shared at SXSW in March 2012, every founding team needs to have three components – you need a "hacker," you need a "hustler," and you need a "hipster."

Whatever you're doing in business, things are going to get hard. It's going to be hard to persuade people and you need to hustle throughout that process. So, one thing that was important to us, and we did it fairly well, was getting our message out in the press. We were covered in influential outlets like TechCrunch and Mashable at the start.

When you don't have a brand yet, step number one is framing your story in the greater context of a major accelerating trend. We pitched our company originally as the "YouTube for Flash games." We had a comprehensive database of the world's best games and technology for publishers to embed games anywhere. That framing was really important to the story since it suggested a much grander vision. Framing is also critically important because it makes life easier for journalists; after all, they're trying to write something interesting for their readers.

It helped that I had some contacts at TechCrunch because of my previous startup. Through Y Combinator, I knew a lot of entrepreneurs. I would find people who had been covered by certain publications and ask, "Do you mind introducing me to the journalist?" Obviously, Y Combinator helped quite a bit; the journalist knows that if Y Combinator has accepted you, you're probably worth talking to.

We did a couple of cycles of media outreach right at the start which was quite useful because we were a sales-driven startup. We had to get deals with other websites to distribute games from our catalog. The press coverage helped our salesperson a lot. We had a couple of really big game publishers get in touch with us. Potential customers in our pipeline would suddenly and magically close once they read about us somewhere.

In addition to getting your company's story out, having a great team is crucial. My Heyzap c0-founder is my friend Jude Gomila. We've known each other since we were 13 years old – a very long time. We went to school and then onto university together.

In terms of complementary skillset, my background was computer science and I programmed the initial website. I still do a little bit of programming. Jude studied engineering, so he had a design background and did the initial design. In addition, he had more startup and sales experience.

With respect to our initial hires, the first person we took onboard was another friend we'd known as long as we'd known each other (a good way to hire). Since then, we've brought in a couple more engineers we've known for a long time.

It tends to be a little easier to hire for our business because many people want gaming jobs. In addition to this self-selecting nature of gaming, another major selling point for our early hires was the opportunity to build this startup from nothing. Funding from Y Combinator and Union Square Ventures also made us an appealing startup for which to work.

Our hiring strategy has evolved over time. At the start, if someone had the right skillset, we thought that was good enough. Nowadays, we're much more focused on the cultural fit. Does this person even fit in a startup? Are they creative? Are they willing to work hard, take risks, and be happy with other people taking risks?

As with any partnership, we have to keep our relationship moving forward. As I said, Jude and I have been friends for a long time, done projects together, and climbed mountains together. We even used to go to the gym for three hours a day. So before we started this company, we had a long history of working through problems together and knowing what the other one thinks. We're very open to each other's ideas. Neither of us is overly emotional, so we find it very easy to resolve arguments. Even if we strongly disagree, we always talk through the pros and cons and come to a resolution. Getting the chemistry right from the get-go is probably the most important thing. That's not something you can change afterwards.

Chapter 20

Riding Prosperity Cycles

In 1998, I came across a book—<u>The Fifth Discipline</u>—that I felt was way ahead of its time. The author, Peter Senge, helped me understand what it was like to build a learning organization. In such a place, learning is valued because it inspires us to continually recreate ourselves; re-perceive the world and our relationship to it; and above all, it's where we extend our capacity to create, to invent, and to be part of the generative process of life. There are certainly no shortcuts to prosperity, but if you start with a farsighted vision, and an honest assessment of your current reality, you'll discover that what's missing is where your greatest opportunity lies. Senge calls it "creative tension" and Mark Hopkins shows you how to harness its power.

Mark Hopkins

Mark Hopkins, author of <u>Shortcut to Prosperity</u>, discusses becoming an "entrepreneurial actuary" to enable the pursuit of one's passion, networking with others who share your passion, and building "prosperity cycles."

Great companies are built by people with deep knowledge and experience within a particular niche. That depth is what gives them the insight to develop worthwhile products and services for which people will actually reach into their pockets and pay.

How do you get that type of deep experience? The short answer is passion. People naturally get passionate about almost anything they take the time to learn a lot about, assuming, of course, that they chose the subject in the first place. When somebody forces you to learn something, it's not very much fun, but if you learn by following your natural curiosity, it's a different story. Start with something you're curious about and dig deeper. If it is something you latch on to, you'll never get bored learning more about it and you'll know that you've found your passion.

The way I discovered my passion was by following the blueprint I just laid out. I was an engineer at Cornell. I went to work in the manufacturing organization at Hewlett-Packard, which was then leading the world in the development of electronic products.

I became fascinated with the components that must come together just right for manufacturing to work. This involved far more than product design; it also included designing the process to mass produce the product. And, the process cannot work without the people who make it move. What it took to build world-class computers began to fascinate me more and more.

I became an expert in manufacturing operations and in working with high-performing teams and drew satisfaction from doing things that nobody else had done before. My curiosity grew about manufacturing at a level above everybody else on the globe. Manufacturing operations is not the most sexy thing in the world, but I really got into it.

I spent a lot of years getting that learning curve down to the point where I knew more about how to manufacture technology products, and eventually medical products, than almost anybody. That's the foundation on which I built my company.

I believe curiosity is the catalyst for passion. We live in a world of information overload and it's easy to just shut down and ignore most of what is passing us by. Therefore, it's important to be thoughtful enough to keep tabs on the tickertape of information that's flowing by us all the time and to stop and ponder when something of interest flashes by. Entrepreneurs figure out how to tune in to these opportunities and flag what interests them. I call this being an "entrepreneurial actuary," which is the ability to spot and ponder the economic viability of an idea in real time. I'll share an interesting example of this.

One entrepreneur I know founded a company that developed workforce management software for many companies, including Wal-Mart. When he first began looking for what he wanted to do, he was in Las Vegas for a business convention where, like many people in Vegas, he overindulged and woke up in the morning with a monster headache wondering, "Gosh, I wonder how many other people do this? And is there an opportunity for a company called 'The Recovery Room' to deal with people like me?" He actually created a business plan which was pretty compelling. Though he did not pursue it, it's a good example of being somewhere and seeing something viable even when it's completely far afield from what you do. It all starts with being thoughtful.

Of course, pursuing a passion born of thoughtfulness cannot be a solitary endeavor. The best way to network, to connect with others, is by engaging them. People with a shared passion love to talk about it. When you are deeply knowledgeable about a subject you love, you'll find yourself hanging out in the same places, both real and virtual, as the A-listers with whom you want to connect. Then all you have to do is reach out. Some won't respond, so just move on and don't take it personally. On the other hand, most of the people who you would never think would have the time to talk to you will get back to you right away. But, you must be credible; show them the respect of being knowledgeable enough to ask insightful questions. If you do, you will find that successful people want to help others who are travelling the same path.

You should not only engage them with insightful questions, but also volunteer your time and expertise. Everybody needs help. A friend of mine, Tommy Spaulding, in his book <u>It's Not Just Who You Know</u>, advises going into relationships focused on what you can give rather than what you can get. It is amazing how often the act of giving eventually turns around and comes back to you. If you start with what you can do for these A-listers before focusing on what they can do for you, you'll be successful. The best salesmen all do that. They don't go in trying to make the sale. They go in trying to understand what they can do for a person. Sometimes this has nothing to do with the product they sell, but they'll do it anyway; those are the best salesmen.

After passion and robust networking, the greatest contributor to an entrepreneur's confidence building is, no surprise: successes – lots and lots of successes build confidence. I call this the "prosperity cycle." The prosperity cycle starts with a single small success and leads to bigger and bigger successes until you look around and say, "Wow, I can't believe what I had the good fortune to be involved in."

To start this cycle, you have to arrive at a point where you're ready to actually do something. Based on the people I talk to, I find that motivation comes from two places: One is a compelling personal vision that is so exciting you cannot wait to make progress toward it. Two comes from some of the most successful people I talk to; they faced incredibly tough circumstances growing up. That personal hardship got them to the point where they were mad as heck, not going to take anymore, and again, they decided to do something. However you get there, start with a decision to do something. Then, move to the next step of applying self-discipline and focus all efforts on making that something happen. When you do this you're going to either get what you want or you're going to learn from your failure. I'm not sure which one is more valuable.

One person I spoke with about hardship says as long as everybody walks away without losing a limb, then it's all good. When she faces challenges at work, she reframes them in comparison to things she dealt with in the past. Winning and learning are both really valuable and lead to confidence that allows you to reenter the cycle a little stronger each time.

You have to go into entrepreneurship with your eyes open. Anybody who is thinking about pursuing this path should realize this means foregoing a balanced and predictable life in exchange for one that is going to have extremely high highs, making you scream for joy, but also gut wrenching lows. Both come with the territory.

Entrepreneurs are by definition plowing new ground, which means some initiatives work, but many don't. You cannot let the successes make you feel like you are infallible, likewise you can't allow momentary failures to deter you from your path.

You will know you are ready when you receive really bad news but you immediately realize that a great opportunity is going to come out of it. That's when you know you've got the right attitude to be bombproof enough to be a successful entrepreneur. You have to be able to bounce back.

I leave you with the final thought that figuring out when to "pivot" is difficult. The first indication that this is necessary is when you're not having fun anymore. The next is if you're working hard and not getting the results you like. In either of these cases, it's definitely time to pivot. Other than that, if you're working in an area you're passionate about, and you're doing it with a great bunch of people, maybe even if you're not achieving the financial goals you wanted to achieve, keep doing it, as long as you're achieving enough cash flow to keep the business going. As long as you're having fun, don't pivot. Eventually you will find something that really lifts the company.

Chapter 21

Tracking Metrics That Matter

In early 2005, I got what would turn out to be a mind-shifting piece of advice from Marcus Buckingham when he released his book, The One Thing You Need To Know. Having bought into Marcus' strengths approach of synchronizing individual's talents with their responsibility, my role as a leader was narrowed to only high priority areas. The mantra was simple; "When you want to manage, begin with the person. When you want to lead, begin with the picture of where you are headed." My team was laser focused on identifying one's strengths and capitalizing on it; for me, it was about learning what I didn't like doing and having the courage to stop doing it. Of course, we had to be cautious of not taking the model too far, but as a team, we never lost focus on what mattered.

Today, we're focused much more on supporting the efforts of entrepreneurs and I can't think of a more important tool than data. Benjamin Yoskovitz and Alistair Croll have added a crucial component to the 'lean startup model' with the release of their book, Lean Analytics. This isn't a book about analytics as much as it is a framework to helping you succeed faster—here's the one thing you need to measure.

Ben Yoskovitz

Serial entrepreneur and Lean Analytics co-author Ben Yoskovitz gives the broad strokes of the Lean Canvas.

I have been an entrepreneur since 1996 when I started my first business while still at university. It ended up being a good business, but a relatively small one. The good news was that I had caught the entrepreneurial bug; the bad news was that I got "zombified" for an entire decade in a business I was not passionate about.

When you stay with a business too long, especially if it more or less plateaus, you get into a comfort zone. We were making just enough money to be comfortable, while at the same time being not quite sure where to take the business. My three partners and I had differing opinions of how we could scale and we couldn't come to a conclusion.

In 2006, after feeling stale for a couple of years and wanting to do something different, I realized I didn't have anybody to launch a company with in Montreal. So, in order to build a network, I started blogging about my experience as an entrepreneur.

People in Montreal started reading the blog. I also began connecting with many different people all over the place. That network provided the inspiration that I could do this, that I could think about doing it bigger, and could raise capital. Best of all, blogging was how I met the co-founder for my next venture, Standout Jobs, which was in the recruitment space.

Back then, Montreal was a city of nascent entrepreneurial activity and home to some really great startups and entrepreneurs. We found ourselves at the center of the wave of investors putting money into web-based businesses. It felt like anything was possible and reminded me of how I felt in 1996 when I started my first business.

In 2008, we launched a paying version of our Software as a Service (SaaS) product. This was atrocious timing because we had a brutal recession that started that Fall. I'm not sure any of us really appreciated how deep the recession would prove to be. I spent the next couple of years banging my head against the wall, painfully learning about the recruitment space.

After being the CEO of Standout Jobs from 2007 to 2010, I knew I wasn't ready or even interested in being a CEO again. So, three other guys and I launched a startup accelerator called Year One Labs. That allowed me to focus on a whole bunch of different companies at once.

In our book, Lean Analytics, Alistair Croll and I focus mostly on technology businesses. However, we found examples of analytics being used in all kinds of businesses, including restaurants and even a comedy festival. You can apply the lean analytics principles and frameworks to all businesses.

Analytics simply refers to measuring what matters as you move toward your business goals. Yet analytics scare people for a whole host of reasons. One is that we are able to collect an overwhelming amount of data and it hard to know where to begin. Another is that data pokes a hole in the "reality distortion field" with which people surround themselves. Founders are not always intellectually honest, in part because they don't want to admit when business is not going as well as expected. Data indiscriminately shines a spotlight on the good as well as the bad. But, if you focus on what you should be tracking, then you quickly get to the right answers to help your business. Analytics work in your favor, even if data shows you things you emotionally don't want to see.

To know which metrics to focus on, look at these two factors. The first is your business model and how you are making money or plan to make money. The second is the stage of your business. Within the context of these two factors, you can experiment with new ideas to try to improve those numbers.

At the very early stage, when you're trying to validate an idea, it's all about qualitative data. It's about gathering qualitative feedback from your ideal customers about the pain they have and whether your solution will address that pain.

Once you get your minimum viable product (MVP) in customers' hands, start tracking quantitative metrics, including: usage, engagement, activity, features used, and value creation. For most early-stage companies, engagement is the number one metric.

Analytics also provide early-stage companies with a tool to learn what products to build. That mentality fundamentally changes the way you think of business. You have to genuinely believe that your mission early on is learning. Yes, things are probably going to take a little bit longer than you would like. Outside investors might say, "What are those guys doing? Why haven't they launched the product yet? Where is the PR? Where is the buzz?"

Learning can be painful and slow; but once you crack the nut, things accelerate rapidly and it will appear you had all the answers all along. When you see a successful company, don't think the company was instantly successful. The "instant" successes may have taken 10 years of work. Even the companies that go from zero to a billion dollar valuation in a short number of years were probably running and learning from another business you just don't know about.

When I start a business, I know I'll probably throw out everything I built, everything I coded, all the features, all the ideas, but it's not out of frustration. It is because it has already served its purpose to help me learn what I should be doing next.

You need to track a lot of things and still focus on the one metric that matters. Some companies we profile had a bunch of data, but were able to sift through it to figure out what was going on and solve their most important problems. You want to focus on the one specific metric that really addresses your number one problem today.

We apply this thinking at Year One Labs. With so much going on, it's very difficult for entrepreneurs to focus. We ask, "What's your biggest problem?" and a common response is, for instance, "I can't get on to a tech news site. I can't get the publicity I need." My reaction is to look at the data. Then we discover that despite having 20,000 registered users, there actually only three active users. So, instead of focusing on generic publicity, the real goal should be to attract one hundred active users.

Chapter 22

Leading Ethically

Harry M. Jansen Kraemer, Jr. is a living portrait of what it means to be an inspired leader: he's selfless, well balanced and always driven to do the right thing. In late 2001, as Chairman and CEO of Baxter International, Harry faced what would become his defining moment—how would he react to the sudden death of several patients from what was perceived to be faulty Baxter equipment? What followed was a rare example of a leader who told the truth, and one who lived his personal mantra 'to do the right thing.'

As a distinguished professor of strategy at Northwestern University and executive partner at Madison Dearborn Partners, Harry has made values-based leadership his life's work. In his brilliant new book From Values To Action, Harry inspires leaders to self-reflect. Understanding who you are is truly the beginning of anyone's leadership journey; "if you don't know who you are, how are you supposed to lead yourself? And if you can't lead yourself, how are you supposed to lead others?"

He wears his humility on his sleeve—"I'm not a very smart guy, so let's keep it simple. Think of any problem you need to deal with. There are a million pieces of information that can get involved in a decision. But let's get above the tree line and ask some simple questions. 'What is the issue? What are the alternatives? What are the pros and cons? What is the best solution?' Life is complex, but you can boil the morass down to thinking simply."

Harry Kraemer

Harry Kraemer, Professor of Management and Strategy at Northwestern, Executive Partner at private equity firm Madison Dearborn Partners, and author, shares his four principles of values-based leadership.

After 25 years at Baxter International (Baxter Healthcare) in finance, operations, and executive leadership, I was very fortunate to have the opportunity to teach at Northwestern's Kellogg School of Management, my alma mater. At first the school thought, given my background, I would be ideally suited to teach a finance class. Instead, I decided to focus on ethics in order to have at least some small impact on the next generation of leaders.

Teaching, for me, has been an amazing experience of examining and distilling the values-based leadership lessons I learned in the 25 years I spent at Baxter, my time at Madison Dearborn, as well as on several dozen boards of companies, institutions, universities, and hospitals. My feeling is that we're here for a very, very short period of time, so we need to focus on what really matters. How we can make a difference. How to set a positive example. How to influence others in a positive way.

The four principles I teach are: (1) self-reflection, which increases self-awareness; (2) balance, which encourages seeking multiple perspectives to gain a global perspective; (3) true self-confidence, which helps identify strengths and weaknesses and fosters feeling comfortable in one's own skin; and (4) genuine humility, which helps us remember where we came from, no matter what our current title or level of accomplishment.

If you take the time to practice these four principles, then you can minimize, albeit not eliminate, fear, worry, anxiety, and pressure. If you and I are two entrepreneurs who started a business, the one thing you and I know, if we're honest, is that eventually things are not going to go well. So, let's decide when things are still going smoothly what our plan is for when we go off the rails.

I believe value-based leadership begins with self-reflection, so I'll focus on just that principle here. Most of us are extremely busy, and there is always more to do. The danger is that if you're relatively bright, you end up moving faster and faster. Yet, before leadership can emerge, it's important to take some time out, slow down, turn off the noise, and self-reflect. Unfortunately, most people decide to move faster, to multitask and end up confusing activity with productivity. Yes, they're crossing things off their lists, but they're not always satisfied because sometimes the most important things remain undone, because they haven't had the chance or taken the time to figure out priorities.

If you're going to lead anything, you need to take the time to turn off the noise, to keep quiet, to calm down and ask yourself these basic questions: What are my values? What do I stand for? What really, really matters? Next, you need to evaluate your actions and, more importantly, consider if your colleagues when looking at those actions will have any idea what you really stand for. Will they have any idea what your values and principles are?

People who know me as a very quantitative guy -- math major, economics, finance, accounting, CPA, CFO -- say this all sounds a little too philosophical. And, yes, sometimes we math majors have to put things into logical reasoning to convince ourselves of their validity. So, I've put this into the following three-part argument. Part one: if I'm not self-reflective, is it really possible for me to know myself? I don't think so. Part two: if I don't know myself, is it possible for me to lead myself? I doubt it. Part three: if I can't lead myself, how can I possibly lead other people?

Small and large businesses, whether private or public, have to be self-reflective enough to figure out what really matters so they can prioritize the truly most important things and allocate resources accordingly, but they can do so only upon self-reflection. As I visit companies, meeting with boards and executive groups, I ask folks, "Do you prioritize?" Most CEOs respond, "You wouldn't believe how much we prioritize. We're prioritization maniacs." Yet when I ask, "What's your fifth priority?" they stammer and stare back at me.

I try to help them by gently prodding, "I know you're running a billion-dollar enterprise with 5,000 people, you must have a couple hundred priorities -- but how come you don't have a fifth one? Maybe it's because you've gotten first priorities, 20 second priorities, and everything else is a third priority. That's not true prioritization. Prioritization is figuring out what is number one, what's number 21, and what's number 51." If you're not self-reflective, I don't know how you can possibly prioritize.

Self-reflection should be focused, disciplined, consistent and credible, or it's not going to happen. Personally, I like to end every day by spending 20 minutes or so with no noise. I take a pad of paper and jot down answers as I ask myself a series of questions: What did I say I was going to do today and what did I actually do? What do I feel good about? What don't I feel good about? How did I treat people? How did I lead people? How did I interact with people? If I could live today over again, what would I do differently with my family, friends, and coworkers?

And the last question I ask myself, because I believe that every day we're given we can be better than the day before, is, "What did I learn that if I'm given tomorrow, next week, or next month, could make me be better than I was today?" If you're pretty self-reflective, able to keep things in a relative balance, take the time to understand multiple perspectives, develop true self-confidence, while still making sure to have genuine humility, the rest becomes fairly straightforward.

Section 3:
Leading People

Chapter 23

Empowering Others

The best Hollywood movies are the ones that most resemble the human condition; they keep you at the edge of your seat because they involve challenge and struggle. Growing up, we all yearn for social acceptance, especially from family, close friends, and authority figures. "So, naturally, when a teacher tells me that 'I'm retarded,' I can either accept and confirm it or do something radical that proves otherwise," says Ingrid Vanderveldt, Dell Entrepreneur-in-Residence. She has risen to entrepreneurial stardom because she chose the latter. Look at her today, and you'd think that she defied enormous odds to sit at the head of the table, but if you ask her, she's likely to tell you that she believed it all along. Her dream is to empower one billion women by 2020, and make no mistake about it, she has a plan to exceed that. Here's how.

Ingrid Vanderveldt

Dell Entrepreneur-in-Residence and member of the United Nations' Global Entrepreneurs Council, Ingrid Vanderveldt, reveals the three important lessons her parents imparted, how her fears fuel her big picture thinking, and her quest to empower one billion women by 2020.

I think we entrepreneurs are by nature people who like to do what everybody else says we can't do. Before I was diagnosed with significant hearing disabilities, the educational system thought I was just a troubled child with severe learning disabilities. I was told by a school principal that I would not amount to much of anything. However, thanks to my amazing parents, who continued to believe in what I could be, I learned three powerful lessons that I actively share with others.

The first thing is the power of believing in yourself.

The second is the power of having great mentors. As a child, I didn't realize I was getting mentoring from my parents. But, that's precisely what they were - people who believed in what was possible and encouraged me when everybody else was saying, "you absolutely can't do this" or "you won't make anything of yourself." Having a really strong mentor in your personal and professional life can make all the difference in the world.

The third has to do with recognizing and embracing your own uniqueness. The term my teacher actually used to describe me was not "learning disabled," but far worse: "retarded." That's the term they used when I was a little kid. Today, it just makes me laugh. It's just so unbelievable they would even speak that way. I was sent off to a special school with special classes. Despite many kids, and some adults, making fun of me, all I heard from my supportive parents was that I was special and going to a special school with special classes for special kids. At a very young age I learned that I was pretty awesome, actually. I make somewhat light of it today, but I think the power of recognizing our own uniqueness in the world, and the possibility that we can do great things, that the sky is the limit, helps us achieve our goal of leaving a legacy in some way, big or small.

My passion for "thinking big," as in empowering a billion women by 2020, certainly stems from the successes I've had, but probably more so from some things that might be viewed as failures, for example, the time I was living out of my car because I had rented out my home to cover my employees' salaries. Experiences like that spurred me to feel that I'm here to make a difference. I'm here to play at a global level. I'm here to create a global sustainable future.

The reason I talk about empowering a billion women by 2020 is that I fundamentally believe that if we're going to create a global sustainable future, it's going to happen through a new set of eyes; that new set of eyes is the women of the world. Setting a strategy in place through my work in business, in policy, and in media to empower women globally to see themselves as leaders and as successful entrepreneurs is a critical change that has to happen for our world to survive.

While it may be easier at times to think bigger and shoot for the moon than to think small, it may not be practical when you're in the trenches and faced with raising money for your lofty goals. When I was raising money for the first time, a sum of around $250,000, I remember an advisor saying, "Ingrid, it's easier to raise more money than it is to raise less." I think that's true for anything in life; what we accomplish is set by the standards we set for ourselves. When you put yourself in a place where you think big, when you are solving big problems, when you are working to create global solutions, you are going to attract the resources to make those things happen.

I had the opportunity to work with Dell, a company using their global reach, tools, technology, and resources to authentically empower women entrepreneurs. And then I got really nervous, because I thought: how do I even present that idea in such a way they'll want to work with me? But, when I met with Dell's Chief Commercial Officer, Steve Felice, and shared with him my vision, he said, "Let's do this together. Let's figure this out." Resources come together when you give yourself the permission to think big and stop limiting yourself by your own fear.

At the end of the day, it's about getting the job done, by people who are making good things happen, be it men or women. That said, historically speaking, men have been the ones in the leadership roles people aspire to attain. There simply aren't as many women in these leadership roles.

Here is where mentoring plays a key role. My mentor is Teledyne co-founder, and founder of think tank IC² Institute at The University of Texas at Austin, Dr. George Kozmetsky. He also mentored Michael Dell, which is exactly why I wanted him as a mentor.

When I came out of graduate school, I wanted to build a billion dollar company. That first venture did fine, but it certainly did not become a billion dollar company. Coming out of The University of Texas business school, I looked around to see who else was doing what I wanted to do. It was Michael Dell, so I sought out the person who taught him, Dr. Kozmetsky. I think the secret to securing him as a mentor was coming at it from the perspective of how I could actually help *him*. How did what I was trying to do help him move his ball forward? How could I be of service to him first? How could I make the time we spent together valuable to him?

Dr. Kozmetsky very much cared about the success of his business school, from which I had graduated. He cared about the success of students and wanted to be connected with them. So many people thought they couldn't spend time with this multi-billionaire, they never even asked him for his time. Well, I go to him and say, "I'm swinging for the fences here. I'm shooting for the stars. I've just come out of grad school here. I know what I want to do. I can help you keep an ear to the ground in the school on what's working, and what's not, and share that with you." And at the same time, I was able to benefit from that dialogue as I was building that first company.

Similarly, when I had that initial "empowering-1-billion-women-by-2020" conversation with Steve Felice, I approached it in much the same way. I shared my goal with him and stressed I wanted to add my little piece to their already big puzzle of aiding female (and male) entrepreneurs. In our experience together, I've made it my goal, and now that of our entire team, to become the number one IT solutions provider for entrepreneurs and business owners worldwide; that's a win for Dell when we pull that off. At the same time, being of service in that way first, helps me move my ball forward on empowering a billion women by 2020.

The most critical element when I talk about seeing through a new set of eyes, and what I want women to see, is that it's okay to be scared when you're thinking about pursuing your entrepreneurial idea. It's understandable to be scared that maybe nobody is going to understand where you're coming from because you are, or look, different.

I deal with fear by recognizing it is my ego talking. Anyone who does things big or who shoots for the stars is somebody negotiating a delicate balance between having an ego big enough to believe you can actually achieve your calling, while having the humility to recognize that at the end of the day any big idea works because it has a team of devoted key members.

Fear is a natural part of ego. Entrepreneurs want to be wildly successful, yet the one common denominator among the successful ones is they've all experienced significant failure. Divorce, death of a loved one, bankruptcy, you name it… so, come to realize that failure is simply what one must do to earn one's stripes. If you want to do anything big, you've got to earn your stripes.

Personally, I let myself sit with the fear of failure. I give myself a time limit, usually 10 minutes, to let myself fully embrace it. And then I go right back to the sheet of paper I carry around with me that lists my goals. What did I say I was going to do? Am I doing this or not? If I'm not, then I tell myself: "Cut it out! Get back to work with goals I have to accomplish."

The second thing I want women to see is that there really are no limitations, so why not go out there and do it big? It really does come down to personal desire and what we want to and can do because we're going blazing our own path. In many cases, we may be the first person who's doing it, so, again, why not do it big.

Finally, the third thing women need to grasp, the essential role of providing and seeking education, is always an important element of making anything happen. Create, and sustain, networks of like-minded people. Dell Center for Entrepreneurs, Dell Women's Entrepreneur Network initiative, and Springboard Enterprises are just a few examples of places that offer many educational opportunities for learning how to build a company profitably.

Chapter 24

Tapping Hidden Talent

One of the great joys of life for me is to help someone less privileged see a better future. In a United States where we're desperately trying to maintain our economic edge, it's a great travesty to see almost seven million low-income young adults out of work and out of school. Clearly, as a society, we're turning a blind eye to a deep reservoir of untapped potential. Luckily, social innovators like Gerald Chertavian are closing the gap.

Since early 2000, Gerald has been on a mission to prove that with the right skills, knowledge, and experience, under-served young adults can make a significant contribution to America's most progressive companies. The foundation of his program—A Year Up—is the blend of relevance and rigor that's necessary for anyone to thrive in today's hyper competitive work environments. Here's why 84% of his graduates are employed by some of America's most admired companies.

Gerald Chertavian

Gerald Chertavian founded Year Up to provide relevant professional education to urban young adults. Prior to that, Gerald was the co-founder of Conduit Communications, where he served as its head of marketing. His book, A Year Up, is trying to change the perception of the young adults his organization serves, low income 18 to 24 year olds, from liabilities to assets.

I started Year Up twelve years ago, but my journey really began 20 years ago when I first volunteered to be a Big Brother in New York City. That experience showed me what was limiting young people in this country from achieving their potential. I saw that my Little Brother's potential was unfairly limited by his ZIP code, his mother's bank balance, his school system, and his skin color. His potential was not being assessed based on what really mattered - his ability, his drive, and his motivation.

I saw up close that we were wasting a lot of talent in a country where we have none to waste. That was my epiphany regarding the inequality of mobility and opportunity in this country. It gave me a much greater appreciation for what it means to grow up in poverty and how systems work together to make it very difficult to get out of that situation.

We have to think differently about who's talented and where talent resides. Almost 20% of all young adults in the United States are out of school, out of work, and don't have more than a high school degree. You can't run a democracy, a civil society, or a strong globally competitive economy if you're going to throw away one out of five of your young people.

It is in our self-interest to engage the talents of low-income, 18 to 24 year olds. The adversities they face make them stronger, not weaker. We should see them as the economic assets they are, rather than the social liabilities they are perceived to be. We should think differently about investing in urban areas. We should think differently about whom we provide opportunity and access to.

In pursuit of these goals, the Year Up organization has a number of critical practices. First, we operate according to a set of principles called 'high support' and 'high expectations.' We recognize that our young adults have come from some pretty challenging situations. They have faced some barriers, whether it's homelessness, dysfunction, or coming out of foster care. They need the support of caring, consistent adults in their lives to help them cross that opportunity divide. To that end, students work with advisors, with mentors, with social workers to help them build the self-confidence, the self-efficacy they need to walk into Bank of America or State Street or Google or Facebook and say "I belong. I deserve a job. I have a right to work in an environment like this."

The other critical practice is working very closely with corporations and businesses to understand what technical, behavioral, and communication skills they need. We continually refine our program to meet these needs. We are a program that is demand-led. After starting with 22 students, we have grown to serving more than 1,500 students a year. These young people are meeting the needs of corporate America.

With respect to "high expectations," we think the greatest respect we can pay to a young person is to expect a lot from him or her. If we lower the bar, we are disrespecting our students. At times, that can feel difficult. Our students earn a stipend of $30 a day. If you're one second late to class you lose $25. So you may have a single mom running up those stairs trying to get to class on time because the bus was late or maybe her child was sick that morning. No matter what, we close the classroom door right as the second hand crosses the hour. Everybody has challenges and the people who do not learn to manage them will not be able to hold down a job in the real world.

In the moment, that practice feels extreme, but we lower our standards if we don't shut the door. Ultimately, we know that our students can achieve at the level we have set. We have to help them get over the bar, as we have done for 6,000 young people so far. We do not accept excuses. We are a challenging environment but our students thank us for actually holding them accountable and thank us for saying "I'm glad you believed in me enough to not lower the bar."

Our "high support" continues after graduation. We keep our graduates connected with alumni associations in each of the eleven cities in which we operate. Our graduates get three things from our alumni. They need ongoing opportunities for professional and social networking. They need opportunities to get career advice, for example switching jobs or navigating their career. And they need advice on how to pursue higher education, specifically how to earn a degree in an increasingly high cost environment.

We treat our alumni no differently than Harvard treats their alumni. We expect them to do great things. We expect they'll eventually contribute to the organization as guest speakers, mentors, and tutors.

In addition, many, many of our students talk about owning their own businesses, becoming entrepreneurs. I encourage those entrepreneurial students to first learn a set of skills, build networks, and get some good mentors. If you do that in your early 20s, you prepare yourself for a life of entrepreneurial success. To that end, we teach our students how to network. We also teach them how to become the individuals others want to mentor. For example, by asking potential mentors: "Can you review the business plan? Can you give me some ideas on marketing or organizational development?" I often say to students that it's easier to learn on someone else's dime before you risk your own dime.

Chapter 25

Trying Before You Buy

A large percentage of the time, it seems pretty clear that what's great for the community is also great for business. Personally, it seems ideal to make money while doing good for the environment. In 2005, the first Clinton Global Initiative brought world leaders, CEOs, and humanitarians together to address ways to produce shared value. The rise of social entrepreneurship is exemplified by Jen Boulden who co-founded Ideal Bite in that same year. Her business catered to the untapped 'light green consumer' market. She quickly grew her company's *Daily Eco* email subscriber base to over 500,000 before selling the venture to The Walt Disney Company 3 years later. This is how she did good in the world while making money.

Jen Boulden

Jen Boulden shares how she put together a committed group of people at her start-up, Ideal Bite – an eco-newsletter company that amassed a loyal following of more than a half-million subscribers.

When I cofounded Ideal Bite with Heather Stephenson, I already had a green business consulting firm. I went through twenty interns and took the top two over to Ideal Bite, so we started with the crème de la crème. Those two interns ended up being our first two employees, with one becoming our salesperson and the other our main editor. They did very well when we sold the business to the Walt Disney Company three years later. They deserved the upside because they brought so much heart, soul, and value into the business.

There was a lot of handholding in the beginning because they were 21 years old and did not yet have the necessary skillset, but we could see they were smart and passionate. They loved green. They loved the business. They loved the lifestyle. They loved that coming to work meant getting on the computer and instant messaging, "Good morning, Heather and Jen. I'm here." That's how they reported to work.

We standardized this hiring practice as a three-month internship program that made it crystal clear if there was a good fit. If an intern was not working out, it was simply, "Great, okay, bye." There weren't any hard feelings or any ambiguity about being an intern forever. At the end of the program, we said to our star interns, "We're really impressed and see a future here for you." If we had an immediate job opening, obviously we offered it to them. If we didn't, we figured out how to pay them as freelancers until we again had a full-time position we could plug them into. Our interns were all try before you buy. We ended up with really inexpensive yet very talented people.

The green business field gave us so many great interns to choose from —Ivy League school graduates who were "passion-preneurs". Their mindset was, 'I don't care what it takes but I'm going to get into this field.' We had our pick of people that were okay making little or no money for a few months of experience.

I did this from the town of Bozeman, Montana. From a personal perspective, I realized Ideal Bite was at a tipping point when someone would come up to me in a restaurant and say, "Are you Jen from Ideal Bite? Oh my God! I get your daily email. I love it. I can't believe it's here in Bozeman." We ran it like it was a national company. Heather was in San Francisco and I was in Bozeman. Our interns were in other cities, including New York and Atlanta.

It was at that point when I realized I had to stop trying to micromanage everything. Heather and I are both perfectionists with really high standards. But, we had to put more effort into training people and being patient because they didn't always come to the table with the innate sense of how to sell, how to write, or how to craft appropriate emails to customers. We had to teach ourselves how to take a deep breath and to have more patience -- to slow down a little bit, which wasn't in our nature. It was a question of offloading work so we could focus on the important stuff. Just raising money took 50% of our time. You can't do that and then fit in the time to actually do every little single thing for the business.

With respect to professional development, we did not have any kind of cookie-cutter training program. It was based on the person's level of confidence and where they needed a little bit more help. We focused our training on the areas where they needed help. I remember when I hired a marketing manager and suddenly realized I had to give up some of my day-to-day responsibilities. She was great with 70% of the stuff right off the bat, but we trained her on the 30% that needed more finesse, the nuances that can't just be gleaned from a book on marketing. That 30% that was tied to our special way of doing things - our special touch.

Again, it wasn't a training program. Instead, we saw where our employees needed help and gave it to them. We also told our staff that if they didn't ask, we wouldn't always know what they needed because we were going a million miles a minute. It was up to them to help us figure out where they had gaps.

Even the voice of our editorial content evolved through an intern boost. Our very first wave of email newsletters was just one idea a day. For example, one day it might on be fair trade coffee: what the best ones were, and how that could help some of the forest remain standing and help keep the coffee farmers' kids out of the fields and in school. This one concept a day we called "The Voice."

At first, The Voice was an amalgamation of just Heather's and my real voice. I've got a green MBA, so I've been drinking this green Kool-Aid for a really long time. Heather has a little different perspective in that she's green, too, but not in the hardcore way. If it were just my voice, maybe it wouldn't have resonated with so many people because I'm more hardcore green. Blending our voices together was a good start.

Remember, two of my favorite interns came with me from my past company. One of them, Toshio Meronek, had this great ability for shtick. Shtick was what was missing in making the newsletter hip and cool and edgy and fun and entertaining. So then, it became a perfect blend of Heather, who has a Masters in Shakespearean literature; me, with my green MBA; and Toshio, who read People magazine all the time and was constantly making us hipper and cooler and fun and funny. The three of us combined to form one voice.

Ultimately, we figured out how to template-ize that voice to have consistency when we launched new editions. For example, we created a newsletter for moms because a lot of women go green when they get pregnant. We launched each new edition and trained the editors by breaking out and explaining all of the components of our voice. We even gave a series of tests so everyone could learn our voice.

Chapter 26

Creating a Collaborative Culture

There seems to be a correlation between the number of people who reject your idea and its potential for success; all the more so when those closest to you bombard you with all the reasons you should *not* pursue an idea you're passionate about. In 1995, that's what happened to entrepreneur Nick Sarillo when he had the idea to open a family-friendly pizza restaurant in Suburban Chicago. The odds were certainly stacked against him; he had no business experience, had never read a business book, and his only professional training was in building houses. Yet his determination prevailed, making up for his lack of business knowledge with hard work and inspiration.

Today, seventeen years later, Nick's Pizza & Pub makes national headlines because of its dedication to 'The Nick's Experience,' which provides its community with 'with an unforgettable place to connect with your family and friends, to have fun, and to feel at home!' It's no accident that Nick's Pizza is one of the highest grossing pizza restaurants in the country; it's built on purpose from the inside out. In his first book, <u>A Slice of The Pie</u>, Nick shares how a culture—even in a blue-collar environment—can ignite tremendous and predictable business success. Here's his formula.

Nick Sarillo

Nick Sarillo, of Nick's Pizza & Pub in suburban Chicago, shares his recipe for creating an energized team by instilling a greater sense of purpose, even when the chips are down.

I wanted to build and have the kind of company where people enjoy coming to work every day. We spend so much of our lives working, why not have people come to work excited?

I was not always sure if I was doing the right thing. You have those times when you question yourself. I had this innate sense that what I was doing in my business was more than just making pizza, was more than just a job, it had meaning in my life. It wasn't just about making money, either; it was about making the world a better place. I measured business success by creating a new experience and having a positive impact on society. I believe each of us has some kind of meaning to which we connect, that helps us through those tough times, those tough days where you're not sure if this is right. You have to be able to say, "Wait a second, this is bigger than just making a buck. Am I creating something that's going to make a difference in people's lives? Okay, I can suffer another day through this for that."

The real important thing, though, is that when I created the purpose for our company it wasn't just me telling everybody what our purpose was.

It was a collaborative question: "Wait a second, how are we different? What is going on here? What is it we're here to do?"

I found our purpose seven years after I started the business, meaning I did not have our purpose clearly defined before I started the company. That is why I say anybody can do it. It doesn't matter if it's day "one" or day "seven years later". We got together with a dishwasher, a manager, a cook, a bartender, and a server and we spent two days identifying what it was that brought fire, that brought passion. That's why it's so sustainable: because it was something deep within us and it's going to be here for a long time. It wasn't just me telling everybody what to do.

What I learned really fast was how important it was to not only train people to be really clear about your expectations, but also to pull together people so that we could get things done in a collaborative way. I hear often that it is so hard to hire for attitude; yet, that's exactly what we do. We hire with our purpose and our values as a coversheet of our application. We are hiring for that alignment right away. That gives us a head start; it makes it a little bit easier.

On a day-to-day basis, my trainers' and my job is to reinforce the purpose. Day one, I'll ask a new team member, "Share with me how you created the Nick's experience with one of our guests today. Give me an example. Tell me how that happened". Someone will have a blank look: "What do you mean?" I respond "I know you haven't memorized it yet. Of course not. Well then, let's look at it, break it apart." It takes 5 minutes.

Once they understand the experience we are trying to create for our customers, they might say something like, "You know what, I was talking to this family and I told them a joke. There was a little 5-year-old girl there and I told her about my 5-year-old girl and we connected. I created the Nick's experience." "Oh yeah, that's exactly what I mean." So that's what we want to keep doing. That's how you start.

The conversations go faster over time. A week or two later, I could just give that same person a thumbs up when I see her smiling and laughing at one of our tables. But it is a daily thing. As I walk through the restaurant, I'm celebrating the team, tying into specific actions. Simply saying "Good job" is not effective. I tie what our employees do to delight our customers to our purpose. Our values are not a plaque collecting dust. They're actually alive and vibrant in the culture of the organization.

We have very specific training we call the Art and Science of Training. We ask: What is excellence? What does that look like specifically? Yes, that takes time on the frontend. It's a big investment, so most restaurants don't do that. But we do.

We live by three things; (1) setup our team members to be accepted, (2) set them up to be successful, and, (3) support them on an ongoing basis. Our trainees will follow our trainers, then the trainers will follow the trainees, and, finally, the trainees get certified in each workgroup. We score them from "1" to "4." A new trainee, no matter the position, is not out on her own until she has scored all "4s" in that certification. Most companies will prompt you to go watch a video online and you're good to go. Or, in the restaurant business, it's "follow me for two days, then "Okay, you're off on your own." That's not a way to set people up for success.

What I like to say is, instead of putting turnover as a line item cost, like most restaurants, we invest in retention through training. The result? We have less than 20% turnover in an industry that typically has 150% turnover. The average check is almost $13. Despite that, our servers have received $500 tips and, on four different occasions, even thousand dollar ones. I believe that's because of the purpose, the values, and the very specific training.

Moreover, the way we hire a bartender, a server, or any other position is the same way we enter into partnerships – using our values in assessing those same criteria with a partnership. We've actually incorporated that in the 360 reviews we do for our executive team. Our competencies are structured around our purpose and our values, and then we do a 360 peer review. I know it might sound too simple for big organizations, but it really works well.

For example, I entered into a partnership with someone I brought in to help me grow my company. At the time, I wanted to have five restaurants across the country. I brought in this executive that worked with Cheesecake Factory and several other big chains. He had a lot of skills and, at some level, was a values match. When it didn't work, I didn't have to fire him. We were on the same page. He said, "You know what, I only added two restaurants. I have not done what you were going to pay me to do. It's time for me to move on." The way we hire and train works at every level.

Chapter 27

Feeding a Hungry Startup

There is an incredible breed of entrepreneurs emerging, and while each is unique in her own way, the best seem to share a set of principles that tip the odds in their favor. Without fail, it almost always starts with someone bold making a big bet—one that creates a more inspired world in which they'd want to live. Then, it's about the relentless pursuit of talent and strategy alignment to make that dream a reality. Fortunately, Babson College Professor, Peter Cohan gives us the Hungry Start-up Strategy, a blueprint for winning with limited resources.

Peter S. Cohan

Venture capitalist, management consultant, and author Peter Cohan shares his insights about the qualities of a successful CEO leading what he has termed the "hungry startup."

I think the most important lesson I've learned is that you have to be able to mint emotional currency. This means that when you are running a startup and you have very little capital to pay people for the resources you need to turn your idea into a success, you need to show extreme passion for what you do. This passion needs to be deeply rooted in who you are in order to give you the energy to work incredibly long hours and to attract others who share your vision. This is emotional currency.

By paying in emotional currency, you actually convince people to walk away from a more established business to risk working for a startup because they believe so much in the vision and the passion of the founder. When you really are deeply passionate about a job, you don't feel like you're working anymore. You feel like you're flowing with a current deep inside of you.

I'll give you an example. I teach at Babson College in Massachusetts which has been ranked for the last 20 years as the number one MBA program in entrepreneurship by U.S. News & World Report. I was having lunch with one of the students and he was talking to me about the clothing company he started when he was fifteen years old. As soon as he started talking, I could tell that he was doing the right thing. He was so passionate. Even as a full-time student, he was running five companies. My gut told me there was a great fit between what he was doing and what he was good at and it just made sense.

If, on the other hand, somebody is straining to explain what they're doing and why they're doing it and it feels like they're reciting a rehearsed script, then what they're really saying is 'I think I can do this pretty fast and get really rich and here is my pitch'; that is not what I'm talking about.

A "hungry startup" is one where the person is running the company because achieving that mission is so important that they are willing to give up a lot of material comforts to do it.

In my travels around the world, I've talked to a lot of people who are not really hungry. They are running their startup on the side while they have a full time job. They figure that if it becomes successful, they'll do the startup full time. That is not a hungry startup. I haven't even come up with a term for that type of a startup, which is only an option if the big company job doesn't work out.

To me, it's critical that the person running a startup has a tremendous amount of passion about the market they're going after and the vision they're bringing to get into that market. In order to get me to invest, there are two essential factors. The first is that you have to be going after a market that is currently small but going to get big very fast. The second is that you have a great CEO on your team. If I don't see both of these, I'm going to pass.

I've seen cases where a person has technical expertise, but they're running out of venture capital. At the point they realize they're running out of money and not getting any closer to closing sales, it's either step aside and hire a CEO who knows what they're doing or go out of business. I've seen technical people hire their replacement as CEO and end up very happy.

Every company needs a great CEO. A smart founder will hire that person if they don't have what it takes to be a great CEO and step aside. A great CEO has five attributes.

The first is to be an industry thought leader. This means they are ahead of the investor in thinking about where the industry is headed. To me that is very, very hard to find, especially in Silicon Valley where most investors were highly successful entrepreneurs before they moved into venture capital.

The second is a will to win. A potential CEO has to have a successful track record. If the candidate is young, look for it in their academic record or in their athletic accomplishments, somewhere evidence of a will to win.

The second is high clock speed. This person must be smart, curious, and wired to conduct frugal, fast experiments. This means a willingness and ability to rapidly try things and then learn faster than other people.

The fourth is being a risk manager, which is surprising in a way because you think of startups as the ultimate risk takers. But, in fact, in order for startups to survive, entrepreneurs who are great CEOs must be great at identifying risks and mitigating them early.

And the fifth is to be good at is being an A-Team builder. This is the ability to attract and motivate top talent through a combination of charisma and integrity. There are several ways to attract this type of talent when you don't have sufficient money to compensate them, including giving them stock options and a lot of freedom to work on what they want within the context of the mission. However, if you had previous successful start-ups, then you may be able to raise the capital to attract and pay for this talent.

But, if you've never done it before and you can't raise outside capital, then it all comes down to the emotional currency I was talking about earlier. That's pretty much all you've got to attract good people. You will attract talented people if they passionately believe in the same thing you believe in and your company is: things: (1) going after a significant market opportunity to enable it to reach a billion dollars in sales; (2) delivering a "quantum value leap" that can be measured in 100% to 1,000% benefit improvements to customers; and, (3) building a product that delivers on the promise of a quantum value leap that's very complex and a difficult engineering challenge.

Chapter 28

Creating a Job to Keep a Job

There's no more inspiring quote about the impact of a team than Margaret Meade's; "Never doubt that a small group of thoughtful, committed citizens can change the world; indeed, it's the only thing that ever has." As entrepreneurs, this has to be our mantra, especially if we're serious about 'making a dent in the universe.'

For two years now, I've been closely watching the impact Scott Gerber's work has had on his Generation Y contemporaries. In addition to his timely how-to advice, I've been most impressed by his ability to tap the collective intelligence of this generation's most inspired entrepreneurs. His platform is the invitation-only Young Entrepreneurs Council, but it's his example that can make each of us better entrepreneurs.

Scott Gerber

Scott Gerber, founder of the Young Entrepreneurs Council (YEC) and author of <u>Never Get a "Real" Job</u>, muses on being open to entrepreneurship, gaining confidence, and remaining unencumbered by traditional constraints.

When I started YEC in 2010, youth unemployment was tremendously high and the dialogue at that time concerned the decimation of our generation, not finding solutions. Today, in freelancing and small business, young people play a key part in the rapidly expanding entrepreneurial movement. While the YEC has not been the only driving force in that conversation, we play a significant role.

As a film student without a business background, I knew nothing in the beginning. Even before I graduated from NYU, I started a "business" that might have been more aptly termed a "hustle." At the time, my only skill was the gift of gab. I became a freelance music producer of videos by prominent artists in the entertainment business at the age of 19 by lying about my age. Consequently, I entered my junior year with a good amount of money. In my senior year, I went bankrupt.

That was my big turning point. On the one hand, my mom and dad had "real jobs." My mom is a stalwart of the New York City Board of Education and my dad is a long-time, successful salesperson. Neither is entrepreneurial, neither embrace the concept of entrepreneurship. Their advice to me, "You just paid a quarter of a million dollars for a degree from NYU, so now go get a job."

On the other hand, I realized how much I learned from my brief foray into business with its "hard knocks" beating. I couldn't fathom putting my dreams on the back burner just to work in a $40,000-a-year job (if I was lucky). So I said, "Screw it!" and I pursued entrepreneurship.

Don't get me wrong. I'm not saying that college is worthless, although I have mixed feelings. It's a personal choice that depends on a number of factors, including your choice of major. That said, one fundamental truth holds whether you're going to be a chemical engineer, teacher, or anything else: nothing is certain anymore. The composition of the workforce has shifted rapidly in the last decade. Everything you thought, every single thing you've trained for, every moment you've spent on your passion may not be of value, at least not in the way you have been led to believe.

Be prepared for the reality that your plans might not work out and think about how you can build something now, especially as a college student in a cozy academic environment. In order to create equity in something you own, even if it's knowledge equity in the "learn and fail, learn and fail" process, you need to be able to say, "I can run a tutoring service," if you're planning to be a teacher and you can't get a job. Think small and scalable and organic -- not a big business. Create something you can make your own. Create a job to keep a job and see where it goes.

I believe there are people born with the personality traits to be entrepreneurs. Traits like being "type A," stronger on the sales side of things, and so forth. But, when your back is against the wall, due to a troubled job market or life change, you would be shocked at how fast you can move into an entrepreneurial position even without such traits. I have met people who would never in a million years have called themselves entrepreneurial, but who figured it out when they needed to pay the rent.

The most important thing I've learned is what I'm good at and what I'm terrible at, the latter comprising about 90%. Surrounding myself with team members to take the reins of that 90% has pushed me ahead. There are ways to speed yourself up by partnering with smart people. Every introvert needs an extrovert. Every back-office operational manager needs someone who is going to expand the business exponentially. Conversely, every person who can expand the business exponentially through vision, passion, and great business development capability, needs someone to rein them in so they don't go bankrupt by spending every penny as it comes in.

There is a way to mitigate the risks on both sides while maintaining momentum.

My mentors and inspirations early on were everyday people, rather than the 'Richard Bransons' of the world. I learned from people who had service-based businesses, who understood selling and could teach me how. These were not "names," just very successful people willing to teach me the trade and craft of their specific skill set. Through personality matches and relationship building, I found the right folks to guide me until I was fortunate enough to have the idea for YEC. In the last few years, my mission has included meeting and asking highly successful people how I could help them, and building strong relationships even if these connections do not pay traditional dividends in the near-term, if ever.

I believe deeply in what I do for YEC. When we partner with a publisher or a media outlet, or I bring on a new member, I believe in what I say to them because I know it to be true in my heart. If it doesn't work out, the only thing the person can say is they don't agree with me or the arrangement is not for him or her. There is no downside to anything I will ever do in this lifetime.

Chapter 29

Embracing Social Change

Nothing gives me greater inspiration than to lift the spirits of someone less fortunate. Americans tend to take for granted the little things that simplify our lives. To us, having clean running water and electricity to power our laptops is a minimum acceptable standard, even in the poorest of communities. However, look around the world and you'll notice that 884 million people lack access to clean water. As a consequence, a child dies from a water-related illness every 20 seconds.

Few of us will ever understand the depth of those issues, and thankfully there are bold initiatives like the Acumen Fund who are 'changing the way the world tackles poverty.' After speaking with Acumen's Chief Innovation Officer, Sasha Dichter, I walked away understanding that 'poverty' isn't simply measured in currency—rather, it's about human dignity. At Acumen, they invest in the breakthrough ideas of social entrepreneurs who are inspired to make an impact. Here's what you learn from them.

Sasha Dichter

Non-profit Acumen Fund's Chief Information Officer, Sasha Dichter, shares how long-term investments in early-stage companies servicing low-income customers yield huge rewards.

I've been lucky to be at Acumen for six years. Our philosophy is to create massive social impact using innovative approaches to finding, supporting, and funding companies. What I have seen increasingly as our organization has grown is that people believe there are better ways to do things. The last five or ten years have ushered in new approaches to solving long-standing problems.

The social entrepreneurs with whom I interact are teaching the world about what is possible. For example, Husk Power Systems operates in Bihar, a state of 80 million people in India with a GDP per capita of around $450. Starting a business in any environment is challenging, but consider the challenge of providing affordable power to hundreds of thousands of people living in one of India's poorest states. The social entrepreneurs at Husk break through barriers and innovate at every point in the business model, building businesses in environments with challenges that far exceed those of conventional ones. It's quite humbling to witness.

Social entrepreneurs have been around for a long time and don't fit any one profile. These are the people who throughout history have recognized social problems and devoted their lives to solving them. These individuals belong to a different breed, like the great leaders throughout history who saw a dire status quo and couldn't sleep at night until they did something about it. What is new and different today is the broader acceptance of using traditional business principles with a passion to intervene and create social change with a much bigger impact.

It is impossible to look at the world and not think about very long time horizons. The environment, poverty, instability are all issues that are ultimately intricately connected. That's why you can't be successful on Wall Street today and not pay attention to China, India, Brazil, and Russia. Two billion people in the world don't have access to clean and safe drinking water and three billion don't have access to sanitation, causing, among other things, disease and high child mortality.

Historically, the mindset used to be, "We use our money to make money and then we'll turn around to make social change." In contrast, the newfound awareness says, "Wait a minute, could we use our money to make change right from the start?" People no longer want that separation in their lives; they know on some level they need to more closely align those two pieces.

Our philosophy at Acumen is not that all the solutions to social problems are going to be businesses, but the extent to which you can find business solutions, have an engine that makes it easier to serve people. If you build solutions with a viable economic engine, the things you build will be here five, 10, 15 years from now. The reason we need companies like Western Feeds (which sells productive feed in Kenya) and GADC (rice farming in Ghana) to be financially successful is so they can grow and serve more people; we need them to scale.

One of the big challenges for businesses who do not currently embrace social causes is to understand how to make the shift. Are they supposed to be doing this in a small corner of the organization? Or is there a way to focus the company's goals in a way that integrates broader social aims?

Having spent part of my career at IBM and GE, I'm partial to the latter approach. What makes a company so important, powerful, and relevant is the scale and scope of its operations, its people (which can number in the hundreds of thousands), and its financial resources (which can number in the billions). Firms have the most social impact by having programs in place that affects the whole organization – environmental policy, supply chain policy, diversity policies – which need to be in every fiber of the company's being. Again, a firm need not focus exclusively on social change, but it can easily integrate responsible business practices in everything it does.

Every business, especially those with a global footprint, must understand what a low income customer today needs, wants, and how he or she is going to interact with the markets for the first time. Take these markets seriously while keeping the long-term view in mind. By this I mean, not this quarter or the next quarter, but a five- or ten-year time horizon.

Finally, we've seen the most success when businesses partner in the right way. Certain local organizations in these countries, but also some global organizations, whether small startups or big established non-governmental organizations (NGOs), deeply understand the operating environments and are very, very open about partnerships. Perhaps as long as 20 years ago, big or small NGOs were perceived as not knowing how to partner productively with big companies. That's changed radically. So, be open to the expertise available on the ground, and recognize it takes time to understand these markets and to build trust. The right partners can help you get there if you're open, willing to listen, and have a long term perspective.

Building trust with low income consumers can take a long time for many reasons, but the primary one is risk aversion. This is especially true for someone living in an agricultural setting. This type of living on the margin means an inability to take any risk, because a risk can mean starvation, or setting back not just an individual but a family for generations.

We often interact with poor customers with a new product that can save money, can save time, can increase output, you name it. The danger is imagining that person as processing the information in the same way as a person with disposable income. If the downside risk of making a bet on something new will literally make you starve, you're not going to consider that product. First and foremost, understand we all have the same hopes, aspirations, and dignity; at the same time, recognize that if you are living right on the margin, you have no room for error. So, for somebody trying to provide a new solution, trust building is going to be a long and slow road.

When it comes to social entrepreneurship, generosity alone is not enough. In fact, at Acumen Fund we often discuss balancing seemingly contradicting values – generosity balanced with accountability; audacity balanced with humility; listening balanced with leadership. Changing the world requires that balance. We need openness, a spirit of giving, a spirit of service. But we also need to be hardheaded. We need to be hardheaded when we see something that seems kind of interesting and romantic but we don't think is going to work based on the reality on the ground. Realizing solutions for access to water, electricity, housing, and agricultural services necessitates real rigor.

Chapter 30

Protecting Your Assets

Entrepreneurs juggle a lot of balls—especially early on; we're continually working to get our product right, searching for talented individuals who buy into our dreams; and most importantly, working to convince customers to give an unknown product a try. We start out lean and ride our limited resources as long and as far as we can, but often, the one area we seem to regularly neglect is protecting the business we're creating.

Unless you're a lawyer, the legal aspect of business isn't what we signed up for, but without it, you don't have any kind of business. Mark Kohler is an entrepreneur who specializes in law and his insights about structuring your business might surprise you.

Mark J. Kohler

Tax attorney and CPA Mark Kohler, author of <u>Lawyers are Liars: The Truth about Protecting Our Assets</u> and <u>What Your CPA Isn't Telling You: Life Changing Tax Strategies</u>, considers how laypeople (including entrepreneurs) can protect their assets while avoiding unscrupulous or sedentary professionals in these fields.

Two of the most important things an entrepreneur needs to get right early on are tax law and asset protection. First off, let's focus on the tax aspect. Be aware that taxes shouldn't be considered a do-it-yourself project. In this area, it's easy to get scammed or make missteps by overdoing it, buying a package, or going online and playing a lawyer yourself on LegalZoom. In fact, my law firm has a full time employee whose sole function is to fix clients' LegalZoom documents.

While LegalZoom has great documents, there is a pitfall to saving a few bucks on a legal or accounting consultation, which are some of the most powerful consultations you can have when launching your business. These types of consultations can help an entrepreneur answer questions such as: How should I structure my business, as an LLC or an S corporation? Am I going to put my family on payroll? What am I going to do for my healthcare? Am I going to have a health savings account? Am I going to do a 401(k)? Am I going to set up a salary or a trust system? Am I going to use QuickBooks? All these questions should be answered by an accountant to whom you can relate, who is forward-thinking and dynamic. For all you young entrepreneurs out there, take the time to interview and find the right CPA.

On the legal end of things, make sure you have conversations with your partners, your vendors, your customers, your clients, your employees. Don't do everything on a napkin; document those conversations. However, do not rely on email to document the nature of the relationship you have with your partners.

A client of mine experienced two disastrous partnerships precisely due to poor documentation. She spent over a hundred thousand dollars on legal fees in twelve months fighting with a partner with whom she had an agreement written on a napkin and two emails. The sooner entrepreneurs stop cutting corners by using unlicensed professionals or doing things themselves online, the sooner they will start saving thousands, if not millions, of dollars.

Here are a few examples of tax-saving strategies, some of which Wall Street doesn't want you to know about. The most fundamental one is how you structure your business. For a small business owner, I suggest dividing income into ordinary income and passive income. I tell all my clients to buy one rental property on the passive income side. Real estate is a key part of the portfolio of every wealthy client I've ever had. If you want to build wealth, and not rely on Social Security twenty years from now, you better start buying rental properties, too. That's where LLCs are great.

However, on your ordinary income side, self-employment tax is a major issue, as it is now back up to 15.3%. The payroll holiday is over, so now we've got to worry about this even more than before. This is where the S corp comes in. The S corporation is a fantastic tool to set up the payroll and take dividends, saving on self-employment tax. Every dentist, doctor, engineer, internet marketer, sales rep, entrepreneur I have is in an S corp situation if they're making more than $50,000 a year.

An S corp is a fantastic strategy for what I call the salary-dividend split. Too many CPAs are conservative on the amount of salary you can take, leaving money on the table. I've had IRS agents on my radio show and I love to talk with them about how we've never had a client in twelve years audited on payroll strategies.

Now for asset protection, be aware that two of the missteps here are the extremes of doing too much without any assets to speak of or not doing enough when significant assets are involved, for fear of being scammed. One of my clients owns four rental properties outright that are worth over half a million dollars, in her name. She had no idea what to do, so she did nothing. On the flip side, another client had no rental properties and was just starting her business. She had a Nevada entity and two Wyoming structures.

This area of asset protection is where you need clear answers and a clear voice on using the right types of structures, like domestic asset protection trusts and limited partnerships. Are you just going to worry about the basics when you're getting started, with a standard revocable living trust? Will you make sure you've got the S corporation or LLC in the right state? Are you using umbrella insurance? Do we need a special irrevocable trust?

When you first start hiring employees, how are you managing that process? Have a system and plan for your payroll. You may do it internally through a QuickBooks payroll module, with ADP, or through your accountant. Look at the rules in your state. Are you going to have an employee handbook? Is it an at-will state? What are you doing for benefits? Are you going to be giving out bonuses? What is your structure for compensation? Be very clear with your employees right up front on all these points.

Regardless of your business's compensation structure, it's important to have regular staff meetings and create a numeric tracking system for production. I stress all the time that employees need to be motivated. I prefer to give a livable base salary, and then reward people with additional compensation when they do their job well. At our weekly staff meetings, secretaries report on how many phone calls they took, how many appointments they made, and what they are doing to close appointments and obtain retainers. Even at the very front level of our office, all our employees track their production and are rewarded with bonuses for a job well done .

Are you self-directing your retirement account? Look at Mitt Romney. He has an IRA worth more than 20 million dollars. You may think to yourself, "He's rich so he has special rules." No. He can only put $5,000 or $5,500 in his IRA this year, and every year. That's all.

So, how in the world did he get a $20 million IRA? It's because he self-directed his retirement account. Instead of doing his business rehabs, his takeovers and makeovers of these companies in his own name, he said, "You know what, I'm making enough money to pay the bills, so I'm going to use my IRA to do this next capital project." So he put millions of dollars into his IRA tax free. So many entrepreneurs miss this opportunity. They keep making money or signing on deals without letting their IRA do the deal once in a while.

Are you putting your family on payroll? If you pay taxes and then give your kids or your spouse or other family members money, get them on payroll, instead. Take a write-off and let them pay for their own stuff. It's not a sham. You're not cheating. You need to develop relationships in your family where your kids are earning the money you're giving them.

My kids know that if they want to go out on a Friday night, they should have called me four days ago and asked, "What can I do to earn some money this week?" I've got a laundry list of little jobs in my business they can do. I probably overpay them, but at least they're earning the money and I'm getting the tax write-off.

Think, too, about what you are doing proactively to take care of your healthcare. Are you using a health savings account or a health reimbursement arrangement? Do you have a strategic plan for implementing the Affordable Care Act?

And, finally, the fiscal cliff isn't over. The American Tax Relief Act of 2012 was just a Band-Aid at best. Many people called it failed legislation once it hit the President's desk, and Congress hasn't even dealt with the spending provisions. We've got the debt ceiling and the Agriculture Bill, temporary Band-Aids, as well. The problem over the past 15 years is that the Republicans have been implementing tax cuts that are temporary and the Democrats have been allowed to implement spending measures that are temporary. All this was to try to get the economy going, but no one wanted to make any of it permanent because they were afraid of alienating their constituents back home. That's where this cliff arose: from Congress not having the guts to do it right the first time.

The bottom line ... find a trustworthy voice of reason.

Chapter 31

Thinking Like Zuck

Mark Zuckerberg is an immensely talented entrepreneur with a huge appetite to make a difference in the world. Although many still refer to him as "the boy CEO," no one will ever deny his footprint on the social web as we know it. Just five years ago, Facebook had only 19 million active users; today, they have over a billion. Their growth is no accident. Under Mark's leadership, they've attracted the brightest minds, baked 'the hacker's way' into a new style of management, and made world revelations possible.

    I happen to be a big Zuck fan, and when I spoke with Ekaterina Walter about how to think like Zuck, it was clear that his destiny is far greater than anything we've seen—here's why.

Ekaterina Walter

Author of Thinking Like Zuck, *Ekaterina Walter, discusses Mark Zuckerberg's philosophy, vision, and professional growth.*

Mark Zuckerberg is somewhat of an enigma. He doesn't like to engage directly with the public, but I think he is the same person both publicly and privately. The reason I say this is because Zuckerberg believes in a world that is open and transparent. Consider how Facebook demands people use their own name and does not allow duplicate accounts. You might be passionate about different things. You might have different interests. You might work at different jobs. But, at the end of the day, you are one person.

There are five things I talk about in Think Like Zuck; passion, purpose, partnerships, people, and product.

Everything Zuckerberg has done, and the purpose of Facebook, has been in service of Zuckerberg's passion to code and to connect people around the world. Everything he has built has been and will be designed around bringing people together on the web. His vision has always been of the web moving away from being built around the content, and toward being built around people.

Passion plus action equals results. You can have passion, wake up every day and have this innate desire to do something, but if you don't act on it then nothing is going to happen. If your passion is strong enough, it will compel you to take action.

Facebook's purpose is driven by Zuckerberg. Four out of the nine years, even post-IPO, he's been the biggest shareholder. What he says, pretty much goes. I don't think he would trust anybody else. That's why he didn't sell for a billion dollars when he had the chance, because he cares about building what he's building. I don't think he cares about money as much. A billion dollars is a big deal – who wouldn't take it in his or her early 20s?

Another key ingredient is partnerships. Zuckerberg partners with amazing people. From the start, he insisted that some of the smartest investors sit on his Board of Directors. Zuckerberg was also very shrewd in identifying and addressing the areas where he's weak. Sheryl Sandberg filled the gaps of knowledge, networking (especially with the government), and even perspective – because they are a different age, they are a different gender, they were in different sort of circles. The Zuckerberg-Sandberg partnership works because is it based on mutual respect and a shared vision.

They meet on Mondays and on Fridays to start the week and to finish the week. They tell each other some really tough things. When Zuckerberg is traveling, he is absolutely confident that Sheryl will make the right critical decisions.

Facebook attracts some of the most intelligent people in the world. He recruits people who may not initially want to work at Facebook by taking them for walks to pitch his vision. He doesn't pitch salaries or benefits. He says, "Listen, this is what we're trying to create. Do you want to be a part of that?"

I think that's what Zuckerberg does best. He builds the team that believes in one purpose, and then he puts full trust in them to create, regardless of their level. In Facebook's "hackathons," people work on projects other than the ones they're currently driving; employees bring prototypes to Facebook's leadership and say, "this is where we think the product should go." Some of the best features, like chats, photo feature, news feed, and timeline, all came from these "hackathons."

The product his team has been able to build is quite amazing. He knew he didn't have much experience with running a company. He knew he had many shortcomings. He hadn't finished his degree. He knew how to code, but that's it. So, Zuckerberg really took it upon himself to become a leader the company deserves. He read a lot of leadership books (for example, Peter Drucker's). He engaged leaders he looked up to, including Bill Gates and Steve Jobs, as mentors.

He wanted Facebook to become a platform. He wanted to tap into knowledge, specifically that of Gates and Jobs, because these are the guys who actually created a platform around their business, around their software, around their tools and around their people. That's the knowledge that he was looking for – learn from people who have already done that.

So that sort of long term leadership, belief, knowledge, and vision of where you want to take your company, where you want to be, and what you want to build is quite amazing. I think very few leaders have that vision and the courage to stick to it in the face of all the internal and external pressures.

People call him arrogant. But, I think, Ellen McGirt from Fast Company said it best: "He's not arrogant, he's just profoundly certain." I think what scares people is the force of his certainty, which sometimes comes off as ignoring others' suggestions. But, in fact, he is a good listener. He listens to people, but he also listens to himself. Moreover, he knows that by surrounding himself with the best people, he doesn't necessarily have to make all the decisions himself. By building great a team, he's going to build a great legacy.

Chapter 32

Acquiring a Practical Education

Much has been said about the discrepancy that exists between the skills you need to get ahead in life today and the ones that earned you As in school. In 2012, the Gallup organization surveyed 1,217 high school students in the 5th through 12th grades and discovered that 46% of them had ambition to start their own business; 42% were driven to invent something that changes the world; and 7% were currently interning with a local business. However, the sad irony is that the older they get, the more insecure they become, largely due to the lack of real world experience.

Because entrepreneurs tend to be independent thinkers, they need an environment that fosters risk, rewards failure, and fuels dreams. That environment doesn't exist at your local high school of university, but it's exactly the kind of culture that free-spirited venture capitalist Tim Draper is creating with The Draper University of Heroes. If you're one of the fortunate ones to be accepted, you'll go on an eight week journey of a lifetime, culminating with a chance to win funding for your idea from some of Silicon Valley's elites. You don't learn about history at Draper, but you do have to create the future.

Tim Draper

Venture capitalist Tim Draper discusses the philosophy of Draper University, his eight-week intensive sessions for college-age and post-graduate entrepreneurs.

I had a great education. I went to Hanover, Stanford, and then Harvard Business School. It was a fabulous education, but it didn't teach me how the world worked, how the system worked. I also realized that a lot of my professors didn't understand either.

I also learned in a very different way. I can read and I can listen to a class lecture, but I learn better when I do things. With that in mind, I have the students at my school, Draper University, actually do things. They have to cold call prospects. They have survival training.

In addition, we do everything in teams. If I were to pass any advice onto the rest of the educational institutions of the world, it's that students work much better in teams of five. If you have a team of ten, it's way too big because people can hide. And if you have a team of two, they don't think they can accomplish enough. But in teams of five, no one wants to let their team members down. Each will work harder for the benefit of the team than they would for themselves. You give them some outrageously difficult assignments and you say, you're a team of five, figure it out.

We also do very strange things. For example, we stumbled onto teaching marketing in a great way, by teaching what we call Future. We don't teach any history here, but we do teach Future, which combines predictive analytics and science fiction.

I think we've even mastered how best to teach accounting, our biggest challenge when we piloted the program. Our students helped us figure out a new way to do it. We made it a group project in which each group of five students has to master one chapter of the accounting book by turning concepts into game show quiz questions.

Networking is a big part of our program. We sent students to a conference, tasking them to come back with five business cards and getting to know at least one person really well. They had to take a train to San Francisco, sit with somebody they didn't know, and ask them about their life's story.

We focus on presenting. The students take their hands-on experience, tell their team about it, and then the team presents that experience to the class. Our students are in front of the class a lot so they become very comfortable in front of a crowd. In addition, they're videotaped constantly.

Ultimately, our students become fearless by trying enough different things. When you go through experiences such as singing karaoke, knocking on doors, or doing survival training, that experience lodges in your head as something you tried and lived through. The next time you do it is so much easier.

The biggest change I want to see in the students after the eight-week program is to be better people. We challenge them in many different ways. We have them try things at which they will be guaranteed to fail. We make sure that they're in as many uncomfortable situations as they possibly can handle. We change the rules to games with which they're very familiar, so they're a little off balance. When they get through this, they end up being better people who are willing to take chances, willing to fail, willing to try things that other people may not try.

We also have a long credo that students recite in their first class every morning, which begins with, "I will promote freedom at all costs. I will fail and fail again until I succeed." By the end, they internalize it and each is going to be a better entrepreneur as a result of being a better person.

At the end of the big project is a two-minute presentation to a panel of venture capital judges. All along, they are thinking of how they will apply whatever they're learning here to their business. Some of what they learn won't aid their business for 10 or 15 years, but some will help right away. Overall, they will be better entrepreneurs who are better able to face entrepreneurial challenges.

We don't spend much time on how to craft and deliver a pitch to investors, preferring to invest the effort on business planning and financial and marketing models. We spend a lot of time on students' Minimum Viable Product so they can get out there and start building a revenue base.

We focus on results. Every single one of our students that attended the summer program had higher grades the following academic year. All but one started a business or got a job. Some people come to the program thinking can start a business by doing it all themselves. Then they come out realizing they're better off helping another entrepreneur.

We have the possibility for a full startup life cycle at Draper University. My son started an incubator called Boost. We expect some of the top students to graduate into that incubator. Then, if the company has moved along through that incubator and does well, it's possible I'll end up funding it.

I like founders playing the CEO role. Either founders are good CEOs, or they are good chief technical officers, or chief marketing officers. Preferably, the founders are a part of the top management in any company; when the entrepreneur leaves the company, the business loses its soul. I am one of the venture capitalists who backs the entrepreneur to the death.

My goal is for Draper University to take flight and be the magnet for the best and brightest 18- to 26-year-old entrepreneurs in the world. I want the rest of the world to recognize this type of education can make a big impact on people and can take on a new life of its own.

Chapter 33

Going All-In

In a recent accountability group assignment, I was asked to discuss my top five, all time favorite quotes and the impact—if any—they had on me. Without hesitation, I remembered Margaret Mead's epic mantra, "Never doubt that a small group of committed people can change the world. Indeed, it is the only thing that ever has." Those words have served me well over the years, most particularly, during my early leadership days.

I have a vivid memory from the summer of 97', of walking into an empty office space in Orlando overwhelmed by the idea of building a business in a city where I was a total stranger. There certainly was plenty of self-doubt and second-guessing, but luckily, I met a hungry college kid who would become the Yin to my Yang and forever demonstrate the far-reaching impact that a small group can have on a fledging community. We had a magical run, and in eight years together, we built one of Orlando's most admired businesses.

Today, when I think of Margaret Meade's words, I think of my friend Brad Feld and the impact he's having on the entrepreneurial community. Not only is Brad an accomplished entrepreneur and a prominent venture capital partner, he's also inspiring the world with his startup revolution.

Brad Feld

Venture capitalist, co-founder of TechStars, and author of the "Startup Revolution" book series, Brad Feld discusses building a startup culture. He advises entrepreneurs to lead the startup community, to take the long view, and to be inclusive of anyone who wants to engage at any level.

I have a very deeply held belief that every city on the planet can have a robust startup community. If you think about it, every city was once a startup where people gathered to build what now stands.

But, there is no guarantee that a city will stay vibrant forever. Detroit is the best current example of that. I was just there to run a marathon. It's absolutely fascinating to run through a city like Detroit that had almost 3 million people at its peak. Today, there are only 700,000 people there. When you run through it, you get a sense of how far the city has fallen. I spent a day, in the company of some entrepreneurs who are trying to revitalize the downtown area – it's incredible what they're doing. They don't believe that Detroit is dead forever, instead envisioning a future when it's going to start working again.

I went to school in Boston and lived there for twelve years. During 1994 to 1996, I invested in about 40 companies. Though most were in Boston, I also invested in companies in other large metropolitan areas including New York, Seattle, San Francisco, Los Angeles, as well as a couple in Dallas, where I grew up.

The notion that you had to be in the Bay Area to start a technology company just made no sense to me. So, I made some investments in

Boulder, Colorado to get to know entrepreneurs there. At that time, people did not think of the area as a hotbed of startup activity.

In 2010, four years after co-founding TechStars, I realized what we had done in Boulder was incredible, but it was not because of the location. It was because of the people and their commitment to build a vibrant thing. I like the phrase 'startup community' so much better than 'entrepreneurial ecosystem' because it makes what you're trying to do much clearer. You're trying to create something that is both a startup and a community across local startups.

What's wired deeply into the ethos of the Boulder startup community is this notion of give before you get. Everybody in Boulder asks, "How can I be helpful to you?" This runs contrary to the notion of people running around trying to figure out a way to squeeze a little bit extra on the margin, or people constantly competing with each other in a zero-sum game where there are winners and losers.

Sure, there are companies that are competitive. Sure, there are different attitudes and behaviors. However, people here not only work on their companies, but they are also expanding this amazing community. It generates a lot of confidence when you're engaged in something that's much bigger than just you.

We built a sustainable startup community in Boulder because three principals are in place. The first is that the startup community is led by entrepreneurs. The second is that those entrepreneurs take a very long term view, at least 20 years. The third is that the entire startup community is inclusive of anybody who wants to engage at any level.

First and foremost, the startup community has to be led by entrepreneurs. There have to be continual activities and events that engage the entire entrepreneurial stack. Not cocktail parties and 'Entrepreneur of the Year' events, but accelerators like TechStars that engage everyone in the entrepreneurial stack, from first time entrepreneurs to super successful ones serving as mentors, to the lawyers and accountants and anybody else that wants to participate in the ecosystem.

The notion of leaders having to be entrepreneurs is a very, very profound and important one that I hope will be obvious three or four years from now. I separate the participants in the startup community into leaders and feeders. The leaders are entrepreneurs; the feeders are everyone else. Feeders are very important, but they play a different role than the leaders. You get problems in a startup community when the feeders are the ones leading it.

Now, it's not the case that all the entrepreneurs have to lead, you just need a critical mass. Looking back 17 years, there were probably a dozen people in Boulder who I could identify as the startup community leaders. Today, there are probably a hundred. They cycle in and out in terms of their level of engagement, based on what is going on in any particular point in time.

Second, entrepreneurs have to take a very long term view at every point in time. I like to talk about 20 years as a minimum long term view. I don't say that I'm 17 years into a 20-year process in Boulder. Instead, I say I'm 17 years into a 37-year process. People are playing a very long game here, not simply measuring how much success they had this week or this month or this year.

I think that any entrepreneur who has a shorter term view is selling himself or herself short. Most companies are not successful in two or three years; most companies take 10, 15, 20 years to become successful. In fact, many entrepreneurs don't even succeed with their first company. And even if they have some success with their initial venture, their second company often isn't successful.

So the arc of the development of an entrepreneur is not just linked to the first couple of years, but rather something that builds over a very long period of time, whether it's in one company or multiple ones. An entrepreneur, or somebody who wants to be an entrepreneur, has to go all in and be committed to doing something over a long period of time.

There are plenty of people who start a company and just don't enjoy it. That's okay, that's fine. But, if you're committed, take a lens that's long term. In the long-view, there are enormous ups and downs, both internal to the entrepreneur's journey and external in the macro economy.

Let me talk about the internal ones first. You have good days, you have bad days. You have good months and bad months. Good years, bad years. It's this very sort of chaotic mess in which your progress goes up and down repeatedly. If you're committed to doing it over a long period of time, then you will be introspective and learn from your mistakes. You will be inclusive of other people and be willing to engage with others and be willing to accept your own failure as well as others' failures. You will pick yourself up and keep trying.

The macro piece of the 'ups and downs' is a mess. Governments work in two to four year cycles because of elections. If you don't believe you are getting anything productive out of government, then the most you get is one cycle before it gets reset and changed again. Big companies are totally focused on quarterly and annual rhythms. You have to disconnect from that macro. Turn off CNN, tune out the newspaper, and focus on something that has a much longer arc.

The third piece of the 'Boulder thesis' is the idea that everyone has to be inclusive of all who want to engage in any way in the startup community. You are not playing a zero-sum game; you are playing a game where you're encouraging and engaging anybody, whether they're new to town, working for a big company, wanting to be an entrepreneur, a first time entrepreneur, are super successful, or moving somewhere else, but still connected.

Part of this notion of being inclusive is that the leaders have to embrace anyone who wants to lead or participate. There is no 'President' of the Boulder startup community. There is no 'Vice President of Membership.' There is no 'Vice President of Education.' It's not a hierarchy, it's a network. The way networks evolve is that people connect the nodes together to drive interaction. The nodes that take initiative gain influence and drive growth.

About the Author

Moe Abdou is an entrepreneur and founder of 33voices, Inc., a knowledge network helping entrepreneurs accelerate their growth. For 25 years, he has devoted his time and attention to helping founders and accomplished senior executives navigate through the complexities of growing a business to uncover contemporary solutions to their most pressing challenges. His work gives him unparalleled access to the world's most influential thinkers, and as such his keen insights are practical, relevant and always actionable. Moe is a graduate of George Mason University, and lives in San Diego, California with his wife and their two children.

www.ingramcontent.com/pod-product-compliance
Lightning Source LLC
Chambersburg PA
CBHW020910180526
45163CB00007B/2692